Practical Ideas

That Really Work

for Students With Reading Disabilities

Improving Vocabulary, Comprehension, and Metacognition

Second Edition

Kathleen McConnell

Judith Moening

Gail R. Ryser

pro·ed
An International Publisher

8700 Shoal Creek Boulevard
Austin, Texas 78757-6897
800/897-3202   Fax 800/397-7633
www.proedinc.com

© 2003, 2009 by PRO-ED, Inc.
8700 Shoal Creek Boulevard
Austin, Texas 78757-6897
800/897-3202   Fax 800/397-7633
www.proedinc.com

ISBN-13: 978-1-4164-0405-7

Printed in the United States of America

1 2 3 4 5 6 7 8 9 10   17 16 15 14 13 12 11 10 09 08

Contents

Introduction

We created *Practical Ideas That Really Work for Students With Reading Disabilities: Improving Vocabulary, Comprehension, and Metacognition, Second Edition* for educators who work with students who struggle to read grade-level content-area texts and other materials. Contemporary classrooms include students with a wide range of reading skills. The challenge for the teacher is to creatively adapt instructional materials so that all students can be successful and have access to the general education curriculum. The overall goal of this book is to offer teachers a resource that is both easy to use and full of practical intervention ideas.

Background Information

In 2003, special education and related services under the Individuals with Disabilities Education Act (IDEA), Part B, were provided to more than 6 million students, ages 6 through 21. This represented 9.1% of the U.S. general population in the same age group. Almost one half of all students with disabilities ages 6 through 21 (approximately 2.8 million) were in the largest disability category: Specific Learning Disability (U.S. Department of Education, 2007). In addition to students receiving support through special education, the National Council for Learning Disabilities reported that another 10 million students were served by other school programs, such as Title I and English language learner (ELL) services.

Both IDEA 2004 and its federal regulations maintain the same definition of Specific Learning Disability (SLD). This definition, found in United States Code (20 U.S.C. § 1401 [30]), reads as follows:

> The term "specific learning disability" means a disorder in one or more of the basic psychological processes involved in understanding or in using language, spoken or written, which disorder may manifest itself in the imperfect ability to listen, think, speak, read, write, spell, or do mathematical calculations.

While the SLD category includes disorders in math, reading, writing, spelling, and other areas, 80% to 85% of students with SLD have a primary problem with basic reading and language skills (International Dyslexia Association, 2007). This means that almost 2.5 million students in special education and significant numbers of low-income stu-

dents and English language learners face a daily struggle with reading.

Despite having a learning disability, most students in the SLD category spend their school day in general (regular) education classrooms. The *27th Annual Report to Congress on the Implementation of the Individuals with Disabilities Education Act* (U.S. Department of Education, 2007) indicated that less than 1% of students with SLD were served in separate environments. About 49% of students with a learning disability spent more than 79% of the school day in general education; 37% were in general education for 40% to 79% of the day; and only 13% were in general education for less than 40% of the day. Moreover, 57% of students with SLD graduated with a regular diploma in the 2002–2003 school year.

The 2001 reauthorization of the Elementary and Secondary Education Act, known as No Child Left Behind (NCLB), brought about significant changes in the proficiency requirements for all students, including those with disabilities. Most students in special education are expected to meet the same educational standards as other nondisabled students. According to the National Council on Learning Disabilities (NCLD; 2007) report *Rewards & Roadblocks: How Special Education Students Are Faring Under No Child Left Behind,* students with a learning disability make up 48% of the special education students in the grades assessed under NCLB. Most of these students are educated in general education, by general education teachers, who use the same curricula and materials as nonidentified students. Therefore, it is critical that these students are able to read in content areas such as math, science, and social studies. As students progress through school, content-area reading becomes more important, and vocabulary and reading comprehension demands increase.

Learning Disabilities and Response to Intervention

Because of changes to the SLD identification requirements under IDEA 2004 and the implementation of a Response to Intervention (RTI) approach, students experiencing reading difficulty are now provided with a series of increasingly intensive individualized instructional interventions before being referred for special education assessment and services. These interventions are designed and delivered by general education staff, with support from special education personnel. Interventions provided in the RTI model should also be monitored, and data related to improvement should be gathered and reviewed at regular intervals. RTI models propose a 3-tiered process of student intervention:

Tier One: Primary intervention is high-quality, research-based, whole-group instruction combined with general screening processes.

Practical Ideas That Really Work for Students With Reading Disabilities contains a screening assessment to identify problem areas in reading for students. All ideas are supported by scientifically based or peer-reviewed research, and many can be implemented as whole-group instruction.

Tier Two: The second level of intervention includes research-based, small-group, or individual instruction in specific areas of weakness.

Practical Ideas That Really Work for Students With Reading Disabilities contains an Intervention Plan that can be used to show which interventions have been implemented and how the student has responded to those interventions. When using the RTI model, it is critical for schools to be diligent in tracking students' response to interventions.

Tier Three: The third level of intervention is individual supports with instruction through individualized programming.

Data collected during the RTI process should be part of the SLD assessment process. Schools must therefore document that a student has been provided appropriate instruction by qualified personnel before he or she is identified with a learning disability. According to NCLB, appropriate instruction in reading must include the areas of phonemic awareness, phonics, vocabulary development, reading fluency, and reading comprehension. *Practical Ideas That Really Work for Students With Reading Disabilities* contains interventions designed to target specific skills in two of these key areas: vocabulary development and reading comprehension strategies. In addition, we have added a third domain that is critical to the success of students with learning disabilities: metacognitive skills. Metacognition refers to higher order thinking that controls the cognitive processes that are necessary for learning. Skills that are necessary for planning how to approach a learning task, how to self-monitor comprehension, and how to evaluate progress toward the completion of a task are examples of metacognitive tasks. Many of the ideas in this book are appropriate for students who are served through an Individualized Education Program (IEP) and for students served in other settings, such as special education and alternative education classrooms.

Practical Ideas That Really Work for Students With Reading Disabilities provides an assessment system and set of intervention ideas for students with mild or moderate reading disabilities or struggling readers in the content areas. They are intended for use with students in Grades 3 through 9 and include two main components:

- *Evaluation Form with a Rating Scale, Ideas Matrix, and Intervention Plan.* The Rating Scale portion of the Evaluation Form is a criterion-referenced measure for evaluating reading behaviors that impact student learning. The items on the scale are specific descriptors that correlate to three general areas that are significant to reading success: vocabulary development, reading comprehension, and metacognitive skills. The Ideas Matrix on page 3 of the Evaluation Form provides a systematic way of linking the results of the Rating Scale to interventions. The Intervention Plan is a record-keeping tool that educators can use to document the skills they are targeting, the interventions they try, and the evaluation of the interventions. We hope that educators use the matrix and the Intervention Plan as tools for selecting and documenting effective interventions to meet each student's unique needs.

- *A manual of practical ideas.* The ideas in this book were written to assist teachers in adapting grade-level materials and grade-level teaching strategies to improve the success of students whose reading skills are significantly below grade level. The ideas were developed to meet the needs of students with a range of reading difficulties and at varying cognitive levels. The book contains an explanation of each idea, reproducible worksheets, examples, illustrations, and tips designed for easy implementation.

Development of the Rating Scale

The criterion-referenced Rating Scale in the Evaluation Form is intended for use by teachers to rate the skills of children and adolescents who have difficulty with reading tasks. The measure was designed to assist teachers in conducting a careful and thorough assessment of the specific behavior problems in three major areas, leading to the selection of appropriate intervention strategies.

Item Development

Reading is a complex activity that requires a student to decode printed text and then to comprehend the meaning and significance of that text within a specific context. To identify the reading problems most relevant to educators, we consulted several sources when selecting items for this scale. First, we analyzed skills targeted by several well-known standardized evaluation instruments that measure reading achievement, including the *Woodcock–Johnson III Tests of Achievement* (Woodcock, McGrew, & Mather, 2001), the *Wechsler Individual Achievement Test–Second Edition* (Wechsler, 2001), and the *Gray Oral Reading Test–Fourth Edition* (Wiederholt & Bryant, 2001). Second, we examined the appropriate literature pertaining to reading.

Field-Testing the Rating Scale

The criterion-referenced Rating Scale was designed to assist teachers and other professionals in conducting a careful and thorough assessment of the specific problems that struggling readers experience in content areas and will also assist educators in the selection of intervention strategies. The Rating Scale is divided into three areas:

- Vocabulary Development
- Reading Comprehension
- Metacognitive Skills

The Rating Scale consists of 7 items for each of the three areas, for a total of 21 items. Educators can use the scale's 4-point Likert scale to complete a rating, with 0 meaning the student never or rarely exhibits the behavior, and 3 meaning the student consistently exhibits the behavior. For each of the three areas, the range of possible scores is 0 to 21; the lower the score, the more significant the student's reading difficulties related to that area.

The criterion-referenced measure was field-tested with 94 students in elementary and middle schools in Texas. Fifty-six of these students were identified as having reading difficulties (i.e., a student who had a learning disability in reading, was identified as having dyslexia, or was an English language learner), and 38 were not identified as having reading difficulties. Of the students identified as struggling readers, 36 students were male and 20 were female. Seven students were African American, 28 students were Hispanic/Latino, 20 were White, and 1 was Asian/Pacific Islander. Of the students *not* identified as struggling learners, 22 students were male and 16 were female. Three students were African American, 16 were Hispanic/Latino, and 18 were White, and 1 was Asian/Pacific Islander. The students were in Grades 3 through 8.

An item analysis was conducted using the sample of 56 students who were identified as having reading difficulties. Before the analysis was performed, these students' mean total scores for the three areas measured by the Rating Scale were examined. The results indicated that there were mean differences by student age only for reading comprehension. Based on these differences, the sample was divided into two age groupings (7 through 10 years and 11 through 15 years) for the Reading Comprehension subscale. The Vocabulary Development and Metacognitive Skills subscales were analyzed for all ages together. The resulting reliability coefficients were .93 and .90, respectively, for Reading Comprehension; .96 for Vocabulary Development; and .93 for Metacognitive Skills. The magnitude of these coefficients strongly suggests that the Rating Scale contains little test error and that users can have confidence in its results.

In addition, we compared the mean ratings of the three subscales for the two groups, students identified with reading difficulties and without, using a *t* ratio. Our hypothesis was that students identified with reading difficulties would be rated lower than students who were not identified. Because we made three comparisons, we used the Bonferroni method to adjust the alpha level and set alpha at .01. In each case, the mean differences between the two groups were large enough to support our hypothesis. The probability in all cases was < .001. We can conclude that the Rating Scale is sensitive enough to discriminate between the two groups.

Development of the Manual

In our discussions about the development of this product, both regular and special education teachers and supervisors consistently emphasized the need for materials that are practical, easy to implement in the classroom, and not overly time-consuming. We appreciated their input and worked hard to meet their criteria as we developed the ideas in this book. In addition, we conducted an extensive review of the literature and focused on ideas supported by data that documented their effectiveness. The result is a book with 37 ideas, almost all with reproducible masters, and all grounded in our research and collective experience as well as that of the many educators who advised us and shared information with us. Our overriding orientation is to provide interventions that will improve access to grade-level materials to students who read 1 or more years below their grade level.

Assessment often provides much useful information to educators about the strengths and deficits of students. However, unless the information gathered during the assessment process affects instruction, its usefulness for teachers is limited. With this in mind, we designed an Ideas Matrix (see p. 3 of the Evaluation Form) so that educators can make a direct link between the data generated by the Rating Scale and classroom-focused instruction. We believe that this format conforms to our intention of providing information that is practical and useful.

Directions for Using the Materials

Step 1: Collect Student Information

Complete the first page of the Evaluation Form. (An example of a completed Evaluation Form for Jon is provided in Figure 1.) The front of the form shows pertinent information about the student including name, birth date, age, school, grade, rater, and class. The dates the rater observed the student and the amount of time the rater spends with the student can also be recorded here. An overview of the three-tiered process of student intervention and definitions for the areas of Vocabulary, Comprehension, and Metacognition are also provided for your information.

Note: We recommend that teachers collaborate to complete the form and decide which interventions to implement for struggling readers in several content areas. In addition, teachers can use the Evaluation Form as part of the prereferral process to document and evaluate the results of those interventions.

Step 2: Rate the Reading Problems of the Student

Page 2 of the Evaluation Form contains the Rating Scale. The items are divided into the three areas of Vocabulary Development, Reading Comprehension, and Metacognitive Skills, and directions for administering and scoring the items are provided, First, *rate* each of the items, then, *total* the items for each criterion; check the area to target for *immediate intervention;* and record the intervention *idea number and its starting date.*

Step 3: Choose the Ideas to Implement

Page 3 of the Evaluation Form contains the Ideas Matrix. After you choose the area or areas to target for immediate intervention, turn to the Ideas Matrix and select one or more interventions that correspond to that problem. Write the idea number and the starting date on the space provided on the Rating Scale. (For example, in Figure 1,

Jon received the lowest ratings in the items related to the Metacognitive Skills area. His teacher has targeted this area and has chosen Ideas 29, 33, and 34 from the Ideas Matrix.)

Step 4: Read and Review the Practical Ideas That Have Been Selected

The intent and implementation of each of the ideas are discussed at length. After selecting the idea that is matched to the needs of the student, plan the implementation. Integrate these individual ideas into an overall instructional design, and reflect them in one or more of the classroom lessons that focus on the particular learning objective.

The Rating Scale and the Ideas Matrix can be used on a clinical, one-to-one basis or used with larger groups of students. Many of the most effective ideas that were designed for students with reading difficulties work effectively with students who do not have the benefit of strategy training. These ideas can be implemented with the entire class, which will eliminate the need to create separate ideas for individual students.

Step 5: Evaluation

After implementation, complete the assessment cycle by evaluating the results of the intervention strategy. By following a model that (a) begins with the assessment of need, (b) leads to the development of an instructional plan, (c) follows with the implementation plan, and (d) concludes with the evaluation of its effectiveness, you can ensure a responsive educational program that enables students to enhance their achievement in the area of problem solving. You can also correlate the information within this manual with annual goal-setting to improve reading for students in all content areas.

The last page of the Evaluation Form contains an Intervention Plan. You can use this form to assist you in evaluating ideas and summarizing pertinent information to use in the planning process. In our example in Figure 1, Jon had the lowest score in the area of Metacognitive Skills. His teacher targeted using visualization, monitoring understanding while reading, and rereading for clarification as particular areas of concern, because these items were rated as 0. The teacher completed the Intervention Plan by noting in the first column which items or skills were needed to begin intervention. In the second column, Jon's teacher described the intervention and provided the idea number she will use to assist in the intervention. In the third column, Jon's teacher documented the time period and how often the intervention will occur.

For example, the teacher is planning to use the idea *Check Yourselves* twice weekly and the idea *Five, Four, Three* once. The next-to-last column states the evaluation criteria in measurable terms. The last column provides a place for the teacher to check whether the student meets the evaluation criteria. Below the table are two spaces for the teacher to list the student's strengths and to summarize the student's academic skills.

Research Supporting the Practical Ideas

Because No Child Left Behind requires that interventions be based on scientific, peer-reviewed research, we have conducted a rigorous review of the literature. To meet the NCLB requirement, we have also linked each idea in the manual to one or more references, including those that used an intervention and a control group, used a multi-baseline design, reviewed and synthesized the literature, and explored relationships among variables. This allows professionals to easily identify the source of the scientific research supporting each idea or the need to implement a strategy to improve a skill or set of skills. Educators can use the strategies and interventions in the manual with confidence, knowing that they are well supported in professional literature.

The following references are presented alphabetically. After each reference is a list of the practical idea or ideas in the manual that are supported by that reference. The references provide interested professionals with relevant information related to research and prior practice as well as necessary information for locating the original research.

Supporting References

1. Balfanz, R., Legters, N., & Jordan, W. (2004). Catching up: Effect of the talent development ninth-grade instructional interventions in reading and mathematics in high-poverty high schools. *NASSP Bulletin, 88*(641), 3–30.
   This reference supports Idea 34

2. Bell, K., Young, K. R., Blair, M., & Nelson, R. (1990). Facilitating mainstreaming of students with behavioral disorders using class wide peer tutoring. *School Psychology Review, 19*(4), 564–573.
   This reference supports Idea 30

3. Blachowicz, C., & Fisher, P. (2000). Teaching vocabulary. In M. Kamil, P. Mosenthal, P. D. Pearson, & R. Barr (Eds.), *Handbook of reading research* (Vol. 3, pp. 503–523). Mahwah, NJ: Erlbaum.
   This reference supports Ideas 5, 6, 7

4. Borsai, R., Siegel, M., Fonzi, J., & Smith, C. F. (1998). Using transactional reading strategies to support sense-making and discussion in mathematics classrooms: An exploratory study. *Journal for Research in Mathematics Education, 29*, 275–305.
   This reference supports Idea 34

5. Bos, C. S., & Anders, P. L. (1990). Effects of interactive vocabulary instruction on the vocabulary learning and reading comprehension of junior-high learning disabled students. *Learning Disability Quarterly, 13*, 31–42.
   This reference supports Ideas 9, 10, 26

6. Boyle, J. R. (1996). The effects of a cognitive mapping strategy on the literal and inferential comprehension of students with mild disabilities. *Learning Disability Quarterly, 19*, 86–98.
   This reference supports Ideas 28, 29

7. Braselton, S., & Decker, B. G. (1994). Using graphic organizers to improve the reading of mathematics. *The Reading Teacher, 48*(3), 276–281.
   This reference supports Idea 16

8. Bryant, D. P., Vaughn, S., Linan-Thompson, S., Ugel, N., Hamff, A., & Haougen, M. (2000). Reading outcomes for students with and without reading disabilities in general education middle-school content area classes. *Learning Disability Quarterly, 23*, 238–252.
   This reference supports Ideas 8, 14

9. Center, Y., Freeman, L., Robertson, G., & Outhred, L. (1999). The effect of visual imagery training on the reading and listening comprehension of low listening comprehenders in year 2. *Journal of Research in Reading, 22*(3), 241–256.
   This reference support Ideas 19, 33

10. Chan, L. K. S. (1991). Promoting strategy generalization through self-instructional training in students with reading disabilities. *Journal of Learning Disabilities, 24*(7), 427–423.
    This reference supports Ideas 21, 22

11. Chan, L. K. S., & Cole, P. G. (1986). The effects of comprehension monitoring training on the reading competence of learning disabled and regular class students. *Remedial and Special Education, 7*, 33–40.
    This reference supports: Ideas 15, 22, 23, 24, 35

12. Condus, M. M., Marshall, K. J., & Miller, S. R. (1986). Effects of the keyword mnemonic strategy on vocabulary acquisition and maintenance by learning disabled children. *Journal of Learning Disabilities, 19*(10), 609–613.
    This reference supports Ideas 1, 2, 9, 10

13. Darch, C., & Eaves, R. C. (1986). Visual displays to increase comprehension of high school learning-disabled students. *The Journal of Special Education, 20*(3), 309–318.
    This reference supports Idea 19

14. Darch, C., & Gersten, R. (1986). Direction-setting activities in reading comprehension: A comparison of two approaches. *Learning Disability Quarterly, 9*(3), 235–243.
    This reference supports Ideas 21, 28, 29, 30

15. Dowhower, S. L. (1987) Effects of repeated reading on second-grade transitional students' fluency and comprehension. *Reading research Quarterly, 22*(4), 389–406.
    This reference supports Idea 32

16. Friel, S. N., Curcio, F. R., & Bright, G. W. (2001). Making sense of graphs: Critical factors influencing comprehension and instructional implications. *Journal for Research in Mathematics Education, 32*(2), 124–158.
This reference supports Ideas 16, 17

17. Fritchmann, N. S., Deshler, D. D., & Schumaker, J. B. (2002). The effects of instruction in an inference strategy on the reading comprehension skills of adolescents with disabilities. *Learning Disabilities Quarterly, 30*, 245–268.
This reference supports: Idea 29, 37

18. Hannah, C. L., & Shore, B. M. (2008). Twice-exceptional students' use of metacognitive skills on a comprehension monitoring task. *Gifted Child Quarterly, 52*(1) 3–18.
This reference supports Idea 18

19. Hecker, L., Burns, L., & Elkind, J. (2002). Benefits of assistive reading software for students with attention disorders. *Annals of Dyslexia, 52*, 243–272.
This reference supports Idea 15

20. Idol-Maestas, L. (1985). Getting ready to read: Guided probing for poor comprehenders. *Learning Disability Quarterly, 8*, 243–254.
This reference supports Ideas 14, 33

21. Jenkins, J. R., Stein, M., & Wysocki, K. (1984). Learning vocabulary through reading. *American Educational Research Journal, 21*, 767–787.
This reference supports Ideas 2, 5, 7, 10, 11, 12, 13

22. Kobayashi, K. (2006). Combined effects of note-taking/reviewing on learning and the enhancement through interventions: A meta-analytic review. *Educational Psychology, 26*(3), 459–477.
This reference supports Ideas 20, 26, 37

23. Koufette-Menicou, C., & Scaife, J. (2000). Teachers' questions—Types and significance in science education. *School Science Review, 8*(296), 79–84.
This reference supports Ideas 23, 24, 35

24. Lenz, B. K., & Hughes, C. A. (1990). A word identification strategy for adolescents with learning disabilities. *Journal of Learning Disabilities, 23*(3), 149–163.
This reference supports Idea 8

25. Levin, J. R., Levin, M. E., Glasman, L. D., & Nordall, M. B. (1992). Mnemonic vocabulary instruction: Additional effectiveness evidence. *Contemporary Educational Psychology, 17*, 156–174.
This reference supports Idea 14

26. Lysynchuk, L. M., Pressley, M., & Vye, N. J. (1990). Reciprocal teaching improves standardized reading-comprehension performance in poor comprehenders. *Elementary school Journal, 90*(5), 469–484.
This reference supports Ideas 22, 23, 24, 28, 29, 33

27. Marinellie, S. A., & Chan, Y. L. (2006). The effect of word frequency on noun and verb definitions: A developmental study. *Journal of Speech, Language, and Hearing Research, 49*, 1001–1021.
This reference supports Ideas 1, 2, 3, 4, 13

28. McCrudden, M. T., Schraw, G., Lehman, S., Poliquin, A. (2007). The effect of causal diagrams on text learning. *Contemporary Educational Psychology, 32*(3), 367–388.
This reference supports Ideas 17, 26

29. Miccinati, J. (1976). *The effect of signal words on comprehension.* Anaheim, CA: International Reading Association. (ERIC Document Reproduction Service No. ED 12226)
This reference supports Idea 27

30. Radcliffe, R., Caverly, D., Hand, J., & Franke, D. (2008). Improving reading in a middle school science classroom. *Journal of Adolescent & Adult Literacy, 51*(5), 398–408.
This reference supports Idea 33

31. Scott, J. A., Jamieson-Noel, D., & Asselin, M. (2003). Vocabulary instruction throughout the day in twenty-three Canadian upper-elementary classrooms. *The Elementary School Journal, 103*(3), 269–286.
This reference supports Ideas 5, 6, 7

32. Sun, K., Lin, Y., Yu, C. (2008). A study on learning effect among different learning styles in a Web-based lab of science for elementary school students. *Computers & education, 50*(4), 1411–1422.
This reference supports Idea 36

33. Tannenbaum, K. R., Torgesen, J. K., & Wagner, R. K. (2006). Relationships between word knowledge and reading comprehension in third-grade children. *Scientific Studies of Reading, 10*(4), 381–398.
This reference supports Ideas 2, 5, 8, 9, 10, 11, 12, 13, 31

34. VanTassel-Baska, J., & Brown, E. F. (2007). Toward best practice: An analysis of the efficacy of curriculum models in gifted education. *The Gifted Child Quarterly, 51*(4), 342–358.
This reference supports Idea 25

35. Verhoeven, L., & Leeuwe, J. V. (2008). Prediction of the development of reading comprehension: A longitudinal study. *Applied Cognitive Psychology, 22*, 407–423.
This reference supports Ideas 1, 2, 3, 4, 5, 6, 7, 9, 10, 11, 12, 13, 27, 28, 31, 32, 33

36. Wang, K. H., Wang, T. H., Wang, W. L., & Huang, S. C. (2006). Learning styles and formative assessment strategy: Enhancing student achievement in Web-based learning. *Journal of Computer Assisted Learning 22*, 207–217.
This reference supports Idea 36

37. Wilhelm, J. D. (1995). Reading is seeing: Using visual response to improve the literary reading of reluctant readers. *Journal of Reading Behavior, 27*(4), 467–503.
This reference supports Ideas 1, 9, 10, 19, 20, 25, 33

38. Wolfe, M. B., & Goldman, S. R. (2005). Relations between adolescents' text processing and reasoning. *Cognition and Instruction, 23*(4), 467–502.
This reference supports Idea 18

6

Additional References

Individuals with Disabilities Education Improvement Act of 2004, 20 U.S.C. § 1400 *et seq.*

International Dyslexia Association. (2007). *Dyslexia basics.* Retrieved May 23, 2008, from http://www.ldonline.org/article/16282

National Center for Learning Disabilities. (2007). *Rewards and road-blocks: How special education students are faring under No Child Left Behind*. Retrieved May 27, 2008, from http://www.ncld.org/images/stories/downloads/advocacy/ncldrewardsandroadblocks.pdf

U.S. Department of Education. (2007). *27th Annual Report to Congress on the Implementation of the Individuals with Disabilities Education Act, 2005, Vol. 1* (pp. 1–54). Retrieved May 27, 2008, from http://www.ed.gov/about/reports/annual/osep/2005/parts-b-c/27th-vol-1.pdf

Wechsler, D. (2001). *Wechsler Individual Achievement Test–Second Edition*. San Antonio, TX: Pearson.

Wiederholt, J. L., & Bryant, B. R. (2001). *Gray Oral Reading Tests–Fourth Edition*. Austin, TX: PRO-ED.

Woodcock, R. W., McGrew, K. S., & Mather, N. (2001). *Woodcock–Johnson III Tests of Achievement*. Itasca, IL: Riverside.

	Ideas	Supporting References
1	Same and Different	12, 27, 35, 37
2	Vocabulary List	12, 21, 27, 33, 35
3	Get in Line	27, 35
4	Line Up	27, 35
5	Define the Word or Symbol	3, 21, 31, 33, 35
6	Math Vocabulary Games	3, 31, 35
7	Math Word Clues	3, 21, 31, 35
8	Parts Are Parts	8, 24, 33
9	Visual Definition	5, 12, 33, 35, 37
10	Vocabulary Puzzles	5, 12, 21, 33, 35, 37
11	Dictionary Games	21, 33, 35
12	Three Clues	21, 33, 35
13	Graphic Organizers: Vocabulary	27, 33, 35
14	REACH	8, 20, 25
15	Highlighting	11, 19
16	Get Graphic	7, 16
17	Figure It Out	16, 28
18	Think Out Loud	18, 38
19	Got It Gallery	9, 13, 37
20	Make-and-Take Study Helpers	22, 37
21	Group Puzzles With a Read-Aloud	10, 14
22	Ask Your Partner	10, 11, 26
23	How Do You Know That?	11, 23, 26
24	You Versus Me	11, 23, 26
25	Get Different	34, 37
26	Graphic Organizers: Reading Comprehension	5, 22, 28
27	Signal Words	29, 35
28	Look Ahead and Look Back	6, 14, 26, 35
29	Five, Four, Three	6, 14, 17, 26
30	Team Brain Writing	2, 14
31	Look for Clues	33, 35
32	Keep on Reading	15, 35
33	Check Yourselves	9, 20, 26, 33, 35, 37
34	10-Minute Review Out Loud	1, 4
35	Thinking, Cubed	11, 23
36	Become a Techie	32, 36
37	Graphic Organizers: Metacognitive Skills	17, 22

Practical Ideas
That Really Work
for Students With Reading Disabilities
Improving Vocabulary, Comprehension, and Metacognition

Second Edition

Kathleen McConnell • Judith Moening • Gail R. Ryser

Evaluation Form

Name Jon Sherman

Birth Date February 4, 1996   **Age** 12

School MLK Middle School   **Grade** 6

Rater(s) Ms. Karen Juarez

Class(es) Science/Social Studies

Dates Student Observed: From Sept. 1 **To** Oct. 16

Amount of Time Spent with Student:

Per Day 40 mins. **Per Week** _____

Instructional Areas for Intervention

The evaluation provided in this form is linked to the instructional ideas in the manual, which are all designed to support students who have disabilities or difficulties in reading. These students, who should be provided with intensive, sequential, comprehensive reading instruction, must, in the meantime, understand reading material presented in content-area classes if they are to succeed in school. The rating scale and the ideas are appropriate for students (a) for whom English is a second language, (b) who are economically disadvantaged, (c) who have specific learning disabilities, or (d) whose dyslexia has affected their mastery of content-area material.

The key areas on the form and in the manual include the following:

Vocabulary. Vocabulary development plays a crucial role in comprehension and is a critical component in reading instruction.

Comprehension. Understanding the meaning of a text—including words, numbers, and images—is essential for literate students, who must continually learn and use multiple reading comprehension strategies.

Metacognition. The importance of specific instruction in key strategies that are required for comprehension cannot be overstated. Students must know about the thinking processes that are necessary to understand what they read in the present and what they will read in the future.

The rating scale and manual are also designed to support a Response to Intervention process in any of the three tiers of intervention:

Tier One: Whole-group intervention with screening

Tier Two: Small-group or individual instruction in specific areas

Tier Three: Individual supports and instruction

Figure 1. Sample Evaluation Form, filled out for Jon.

(continues)

Rating Scale

DIRECTIONS

❶ Use the following scale to circle the appropriate number:

0 = *Never or rarely exhibits the behavior*

1 = *Sometimes exhibits the behavior*

2 = *Frequently exhibits the behavior*

3 = *Consistently exhibits the behavior*

❷ Total the ratings in each of the areas, and record them in the Total box.

❸ Put a check mark in the circle in the Immediate Intervention column by the areas with the lowest scores.

❹ For each area checked, select up to three ideas from the Ideas Matrix on page 3. Write the idea number and start date for each idea in the blanks provided in the last column.

BEHAVIOR	RATING	TOTAL	IMMEDIATE INTERVENTION	IDEA NUMBER; START DATE
	Never/Rarely Sometimes Frequently Consistently			

Vocabulary Development

1 Uses a rich and varied vocabulary	0 ① 2 3			___ _____
2 Learns new words incidentally	0 ① 2 3			___ _____
3 Identifies different parts of words (e.g., prefix)	0 ① 2 3			___ _____
4 Identifies synonyms of words	0 1 ② 3	9	○	___ _____
5 Identifies antonyms of words	0 1 ② 3			___ _____
6 Uses a dictionary or glossary independently	0 ① 2 3			___ _____
7 Figures out what words mean through context	0 ① 2 3			___ _____

Reading Comprehension

1 Answers factual questions about the reading	0 1 ② 3			___ _____
2 Accurately summarizes a reading	0 1 ② 3			___ _____
3 Retells information from a reading with accuracy	0 1 ② 3			___ _____
4 Identifies the key ideas of a reading	0 1 ② 3	11	○	___ _____
5 Makes predictions before and during reading	0 ① 2 3			___ _____
6 Draws inferences from a reading	⓪ 1 2 3			___ _____
7 Reaches conclusions from a reading	0 1 ② 3			___ _____

Metacognitive Skills

1 Connects prior experiences to a reading	0 ① 2 3			33 10–30
2 Reads for a purpose	0 ① 2 3			29 10–30
3 Visualizes as he or she reads	⓪ 1 2 3			34 11–15
4 Monitors understanding as he or she reads	⓪ 1 2 3	4	✓	___ _____
5 Asks questions about the reading	0 ① 2 3			___ _____
6 Rereads for clarification	⓪ 1 2 3			___ _____
7 Connects different parts of the reading to build meaning	0 ① 2 3			___ _____

Figure 1. Continued.

Ideas Matrix

Ideas	Vocabulary Development							Reading Comprehension							Metacognitive Skills						
	1	2	3	4	5	6	7	1	2	3	4	5	6	7	1	2	3	4	5	6	7
1 Same and Different	•			•	•																
2 Vocabulary List	•		•	•	•	•															
3 Get in Line	•			•																	
4 Line Up	•			•																	
5 Define the Word or Symbol	•	•				•	•														
6 Math Vocabulary Games		•		•																	
7 Math Word Clues	•			•																	
8 Parts Are Parts			•				•								•						
9 Visual Definition	•			•													•				
10 Vocabulary Puzzles	•	•					•														
11 Dictionary Games	•	•	•	•	•	•															
12 Three Clues	•	•																			
13 Graphic Organizers: Vocabulary	•	•																			
14 REACH							•					•	•								
15 Highlighting	•	•					•	•			•			•	•		•				
16 Get Graphic								•			•			•							
17 Figure It Out								•			•			•							
18 Think Out Loud											•	•	•				•		•		•
19 Got It Gallery								•	•					•			•				•
20 Make-and-Take Study Helpers	•				•	•								•			•				•
21 Group Puzzles With a Read-Aloud	•		•	•		•	•									•		•	•	•	
22 Ask Your Partner								•						•				•	•		
23 How Do You Know That?								•	•		•			•		•					
24 You Versus Me								•	•	•				•							
25 Get Different								•	•	•	•			•	•		•	•			•
26 Graphic Organizers: Comprehension								•	•		•			•							
27 Signal Words							•						•					•	•		•
28 Look Ahead and Look Back		•		•			•	•	•		•										
29 Five, Four, Three								•	•	•	•	•	•	•	•		(•)	(•)	•		•
30 Team Brain Writing															•	•					
31 Look for Clues					•										•		•	•			•
32 Keep On Reading	•	•					•								•		•	•			•
33 Check Yourselves												•	•		•	•	(•)	(•)	•		•
34 10-Minute Review Out Loud										•		•						•		(•)	•
35 Thinking, Cubed								•	•	•	•	•	•	•	•	•				•	
36 Become a Techie	•	•	•	•	•	•	•	•	•	•	•	•	•	•	•	•	•	•	•	•	•
37 Graphic Organizers: Metacognition															•	•	•	•	•	•	•

Figure 1. Continued.

(continues)

Intervention Plan

	Skill	Intervention/ Idea Number	Time Period	Evaluation Criteria	Criteria Met? Yes	Criteria Met? No
❶	Visualizes as he reads	Evaluate visualization skill Idea __33__	10-30 through 12-10 twice weekly	• Will complete Self-Check twice weekly • Reading comprehension scores will increase by 3%	☐ ☐	☐ ☐
❷	Monitors understanding as he reads	Answer text questions with increased accuracy Idea __29__	10-30	• Will complete Five, Four, Three form • Will attain a score of at least 75 on test	☐ ☐	☐ ☐
❸	Rereads for clarification	Improve summarization skill by rereading text Idea __34__	11-15	• Will contribute one idea during activity • Will use summary information to study for exam	☐ ☐	☐ ☐
❹		Idea ___		•	☐	☐
❺		Idea ___		•	☐	☐

Additional Information

What are the student's strengths that could be used in designing interventions?

Jon is motivated to learn. He has a good oral vocabulary.

Provide a summary of the student's academic skills.

Jon lacks metacognitive skills to assist him in his reading comprehension. Although his oral vocabulary is above grade level, he does not translate that to his reading vocabulary.

Figure 1. Continued.

Idea 1
Same and Different

Strategies that link new vocabulary words to synonyms and contrast them with antonyms can make learning easier for many students with learning disabilities. The Same and Different form is a tool that can help students as they master vocabulary, which is necessary for reading comprehension. Students can use this form as a study guide, or they can transfer individual words to the Vocabulary List, provided in Idea 2.

Here is how to use the form.

❶ When introducing new vocabulary, provide students with an example of the word in context, tell them the definition, and show them an illustration of the word (e.g., project an illustration from an Internet Web site, point out photographs or drawings in the text or supplemental texts, draw an object yourself, or ask a student to share an illustration). Ask students to complete the information in the box at the top of the page as you give the definition and the visual example.

❷ Ask students to provide the class with a word that has a similar meaning. Write this *synonym* on the "It is almost the SAME as" line.

❸ Provide students with an *antonym,* or word with an opposite meaning. Write this word on the "It is DIFFERENT from" line.

Same and Different

The new word is

_____

It means

_____

It looks like

 It is almost the SAME as _____

 It is DIFFERENT from _____

Idea 1

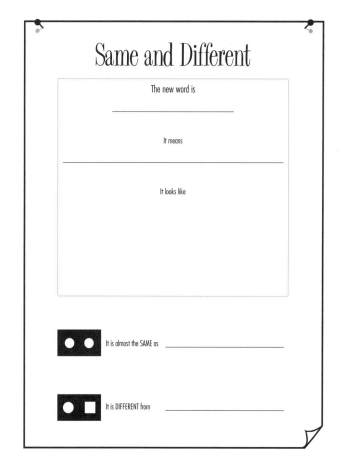

15

Idea 1

Idea 2
Vocabulary List

To help students master unfamiliar vocabulary, teachers should use a variety of graphic organizers and other study tools. Students can familiarize themselves with each tool, practice using them in class, and eventually find a strategy that works best for them. Although many formats help students as they study and memorize new vocabulary, we like this Vocabulary List—it is clear, simple, and easy for students to use.

Here is how the Vocabulary List works.

❶ When a new vocabulary word is presented, each student should record the word, its part of speech (POS), a synonym, an antonym, the definition, and a sentence that includes the word.

❷ The student should also draw a small picture or symbol that represents the word's meaning in the circle to the left of the word. Using a visual cue is a well-documented strategy for improving mastery of information. If students are not confident of their drawings, let them copy one the teacher or another student has done. Make sure each student understands the relationship between the word and the drawing before assigning independent work or allowing them to study with a partner.

❸ After completing the Vocabulary List for 3 to 6 words, teach students to study the list by folding his or her paper into three sections. The first fold should be to the right of the picture circle, so that the student sees only the illustration and (hopefully) knows the word immediately. The second fold should be after the middle section, so that the student sees everything but the definition (the student should be able to provide the definition once all of that information is exposed). Finally, by unfolding the last section, the student can see the definition.

Note. This idea is adapted and used with permission of Hallsville High School, Hallsville, TX.

Vocabulary List

Word _____

POS _____

Synonym _____

Antonym _____

Sentence _____

_____

Definition

_____

_____

_____

_____

_____

Word _____

POS _____

Synonym _____

Antonym _____

Sentence _____

_____

Definition

_____

_____

_____

_____

_____

Word _____

POS _____

Synonym _____

Antonym _____

Sentence _____

_____

Definition

_____

_____

_____

_____

_____

Idea 2

Idea 3
Get in Line

Students can learn unknown words by connecting them with known words that have similar meanings—that is, by forming associations. Get in Line is an effective method to help students form associations by finding synonyms for the new vocabulary words.

Here is how to use Get in Line.

❶ Introduce the new vocabulary words at the beginning of a unit. Write each new vocabulary word on a Get in Line card, and attach the card to a string, leaving room for additional cards underneath each new word. Place blank Get in Line cards and strings in an easy-to-reach location in the classroom. Tell students to add synonyms to the strings of cards for each of the new vocabulary words.

❷ During the week, students can pick up a Get in Line card and write a synonym of the target word. Each student should write his or her name on the back of the card.

❸ After filling out the Get in Line card, the student can tie, staple, or tape the word to the appropriate string. As part of the week's routine, the teacher should read and review the string of words daily, discussing how each word in the string is a synonym of the target word.

Get in Line

indignant

Get in Line

offended

Get in Line

annoyed

🕷 Tips:

⊙ At the end of the unit of study, students receive participation points for each word they have added to the strings.

⊙ Laminate the cards, punch holes in the top and bottom, and have students connect them with bent paper clips.

19

Get in Line

Get in Line

Get in Line

Idea 3

Idea 4
Line Up

Students can learn unknown words by connecting them with known words that have similar meanings—that is, by forming associations. For example, by presenting, writing, and pronouncing new words when they begin a new unit of instruction, teachers help students retain those words. Another simple but effective way to help students form associations is to use the Line Up strategy, which is based on the close relationships among words with similar meanings.

Here is how to use Line Up.

❶ Give students a copy of the Line Up form. Either project the form or create a large version of the Line Up form, using chart paper.

❷ Model the process by showing the student a word. Say the word, spell it, write it by itself on the board or overhead, tell students the meaning of the word, and repeat it.

❸ Write the word in the middle box on the form.

❹ Tell the students another word that has a meaning similar to the first word. Spell the second word, write it on the projected image or chart paper, tell the students the meaning, and repeat it. If your second word is less intense or of less magnitude than the first word, write it in the box to the left of the center box. If your second word is more intense or of greater magnitude than the original word, write it in the box to the right of the center box.

❺ Discuss the relationship between the two words. Emphasize that the two words mean almost the same thing.

❻ Tell the students a third word that is similar to the first word. Discuss where the word would be placed in the lineup, according to its intensity or magnitude. Talk about how the words are related.

❼ Explain to students that sometimes words are so close in meaning that it might be difficult to arrange them. If students disagree with the arrangement, ask them to provide complete definitions of each word and justify their opinions.

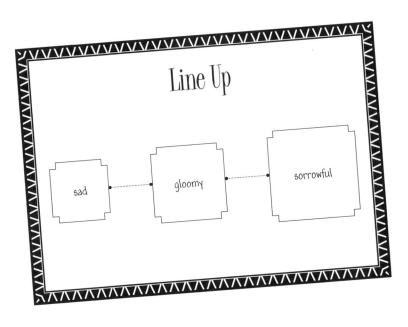

22

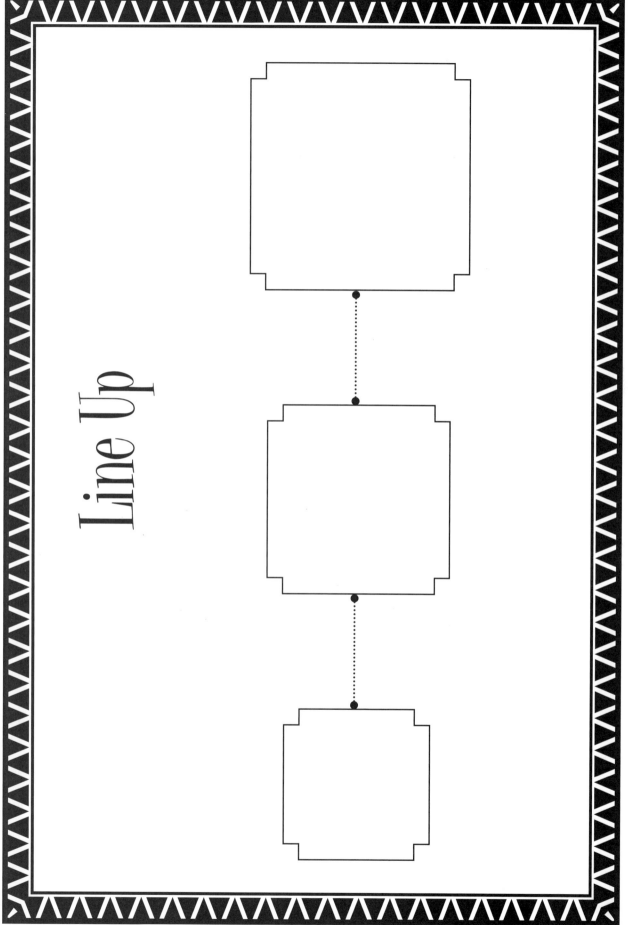

Line Up

Idea 5
Define the Word or Symbol

Understanding and using correct vocabulary and symbols is critical for good problem solving. We suggest two practical strategies that can be used on an ongoing basis to help your students learn new vocabulary and symbols:

- ⊙ Word Walls
- ⊙ Student Word Folder

Both of these strategies are simple to implement and require few materials. You can even use both at the same time.

To use Define the Word or Symbol, follow these directions.

Word Walls

❶ To create a word wall, clear a large space on a blank wall.

❷ Write the letters in alphabetical order on a chart or on cards that are attached directly to the wall. Include an additional card for symbols.

❸ As words or symbols are introduced or used, place them (also on cards) under the letter that is the same as the first letter of the word or under the symbol card.

❹ Continue to add to the word wall lists throughout the year.

Student Word Folders

❶ Give each student a copy of the Define the Word or Symbol worksheet to keep in his or her word folder.

❷ Complete the worksheet as a group the first several times by identifying new vocabulary or symbols in problems or from the text.

❸ Write the new words or symbols in column one; write the text or dictionary definition of the word or symbol in column two; rewrite the definition using the students' own words in column three.

❹ Have students complete the worksheets independently, once they understand the directions.

Note. This idea is from *Practical Ideas That Really Work for Teaching Math Problem Solving* (pp. 51–55), by G. R. Ryser, J. R. Patton, E. A. Polloway, and K. McConnell, 2006, Austin, TX: PRO-ED, Inc. Copyright 2006 by PRO-ED, Inc. Reprinted with permission.

Define the Word or Symbol

Word or Symbol	Definition	Definition in Your Own Words
rational number	A number that can be put in the form $\frac{a}{b}$, where a and b are integers and $b \neq 0$.	Any two integers that can be divided (divisor $\neq$ 0): $\frac{1}{2}, \frac{-8}{5}, \frac{3}{1}$
reciprocal	The rational number that multiplies r ($r \neq 0$) to give $\frac{1}{r} \cdot r = 1$.	Two rational numbers that equal 1 when multiplied: $\frac{2}{3} \cdot \frac{3}{2} = \frac{6}{6} = 1$
ratio	Quotient of two numbers: $\frac{a}{b}$	Two numbers that are divided: $\frac{3}{4}$
proportion	Equality between two ratios: $\frac{a}{b} = \frac{c}{d}$	Two fractions that are equal: $\frac{1}{2} = \frac{5}{10}$

Define the Word or Symbol

Word or Symbol	Definition	Definition in Your Own Words

Idea 5

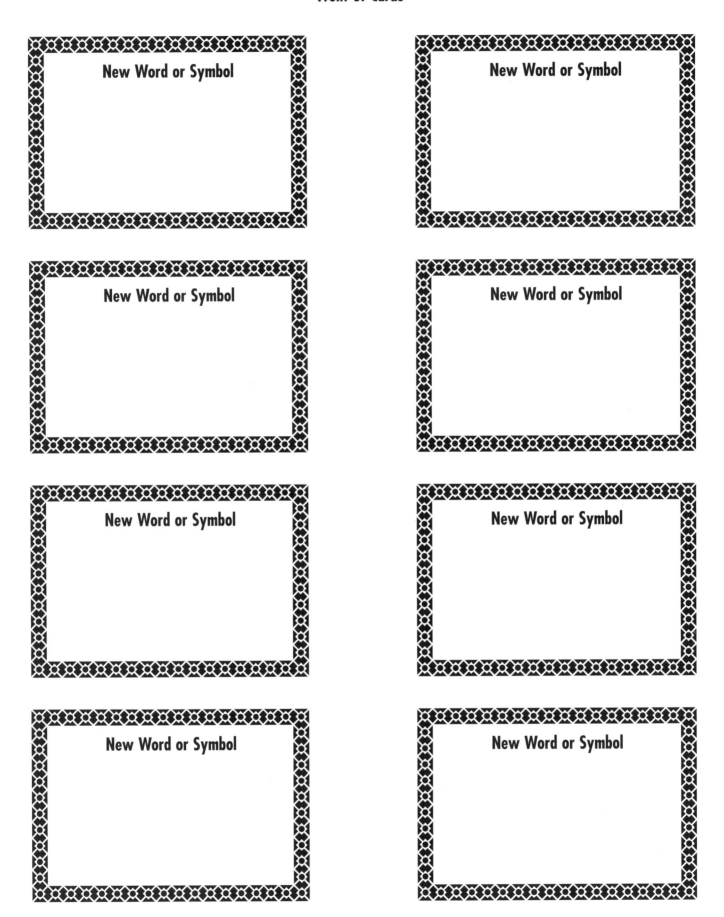

New Word or Symbol

New Word or Symbol

New Word or Symbol

New Word or Symbol

New Word or Symbol

New Word or Symbol

New Word or Symbol

New Word or Symbol

Idea 5

Back of Cards

My Definition or Illustration

My Definition or Illustration

My Definition or Illustration

My Definition or Illustration

My Definition or Illustration

My Definition or Illustration

My Definition or Illustration

My Definition or Illustration

Idea 5

Idea 6
Math Vocabulary Games

Many students have problems understanding math vocabulary, and so it would be beneficial to them if they could practice it in structured situations. An effective way to teach math vocabulary is through the use of vocabulary card-deck games. Here are three simple vocabulary games that are familiar to most students.

Game 1: Fishing for Words
This game works best with at least 10 vocabulary words.

❶ Before beginning the lesson, write the vocabulary words on copies of the blank card templates (provided), and make four copies of each card. Put all the cards together into a deck and shuffle.

❷ Divide the students in to groups of four, and choose a dealer to deal five cards to each student in the group. Scatter the remaining cards facedown in the center of the table (or floor or wherever the game is being played).

❸ The student to the dealer's left begins by picking one word from his or her cards, saying it aloud, and giving a brief definition of it. If the student defines the word correctly, he or she can then ask any student in the group to "Give me all of (the specific word)." If the student does not define the word correctly, he or she loses the turn.

❹ Students who are asked must give up their word cards if they have them; if they do not have the word card, they direct the student who asked to "go fish" in the center pile.

❺ The student can keep asking other students for cards until they are unable to define a word or until the person to whom they ask for a card tells them to "go fish."

❻ The sequence is repeated until someone has no cards left. The student with the most sets (of four cards that have the same word) wins.

 **Tip:**

These games can be modified to focus just on word recognition, if needed.

Note. This idea is from *Practical Ideas That Really Work for Teaching Math Problem Solving* (pp. 57–62), by and G. R. Ryser, J. R. Patton, E. A. Polloway, and K. McConnell, 2006, Austin, TX: PRO-ED, Inc. Copyright 2006 by PRO-ED, Inc. Reprinted with permission.

Game 2: Word Match

This game can be played with the entire class or in small groups.

❶ Put the students in small groups, and give each group the same set of 6 to 10 vocabulary word cards.

❷ The *leader* (the teacher or a student) gives a clue to the meaning of the vocabulary word by saying a word or phrase that is associated with it. (Note: A sheet of paper can be prepared ahead of time with the vocabulary words, key phrases, and the complete definitions.)

❸ The first group to associate the clue with the correct vocabulary word turns in their card with the word.

❹ The first group to run out of cards wins.

Game 3: Word Concentration

This game is designed for pairs of students.

❶ Develop two card decks: One with the vocabulary word and the other with the definitions. (Note: The backside of each deck should be blank or have some type of design.) We have provided a sample of word cards and definition cards along with a design for the backs.

❷ Place the cards on a table or on the floor in a quiet area.

❸ Two students place the cards (the vocabulary and its matching definition) facedown and scramble the cards.

❹ Player 1 turns over two cards. If the cards match (a match is a vocabulary word and its corresponding definition) and Player 1 identifies it as a match, he or she takes the two cards and may take another turn. If the cards do not match, it becomes Player 2's turn.

❺ Play continues until all cards are matched.

❻ At the end of the game, the player with the most pairs of cards wins.

decimal number

numerator

factor

denominator

integer

ratio

fraction

reciprocal

Idea 6

a number written
to base 10

In the fraction $\frac{x}{y}$,
x is the _____.

an exact divisor
of a number

In the fraction $\frac{x}{y}$,
y is the _____.

positive and
negative whole
numbers and zero

the quotient of
two numbers

an expression of
the form $\frac{x}{y}$

For a number x, the
_____ is $\frac{x}{y}$

Blank Cards

Idea 7
Math Word Clues

Key words in math problems provide students with clues about how to solve them. Many students can perform an algorithm when it is presented in isolation (e.g., 2 + 2) but become confused when it is presented with a word problem that must be solved using that same algorithm. This idea presents a method to teach students how to solve problems by looking for key words; these words often indicate the operation students should use to solve the problem. Cards with key words are provided for addition, subtraction, multiplication, and division. There is also a page of blank cards that you and your students can use to add words to each set.

Here's how it works.

❶ Copy and laminate one card for each student that matches the operation you are teaching (addition, subtraction, multiplication, division).

❷ Give each student the first card.

❸ Present two or three word problems that use the first key word, and solve them as a group.

❹ Have students solve additional problems, highlighting the key words each time.

Try these variations.

Game

Divide the class into groups of three or four students. Give each group the four operation cards (addition, subtraction, multiplication, and division) that are provided at the end of this idea. Project a word problem containing a word clue. Have the group raise the card that shows the operation that should be used to solve the problem. If desired, 1 point can be awarded to the group that raises the correct card first.

Note. Sometimes key words do not lead to the operation under which they are listed in this idea. As students become more proficient math problem solvers, move away from this strategy.

This idea is from *Practical Ideas That Really Work for Teaching Math Problem Solving* (pp. 63–72), by G. R. Ryser, J. R. Patton, E. A. Polloway, and K. McConnell, 2006, Austin, TX: PRO-ED, Inc. Copyright 2006 by PRO-ED, Inc. Reprinted with permission.

Center

Copy and laminate one set of clue words. Include several word problems that already have the clue words highlighted, and include several more that have clue words that the student must highlight. Have the student make up one or more problems using the clue words.

Chart

Post the Operation Word Clues chart or provide a copy to each student. Encourage students to add new word clues under the appropriate headings. As reinforcement, allow students to use their charts during tests.

Addition

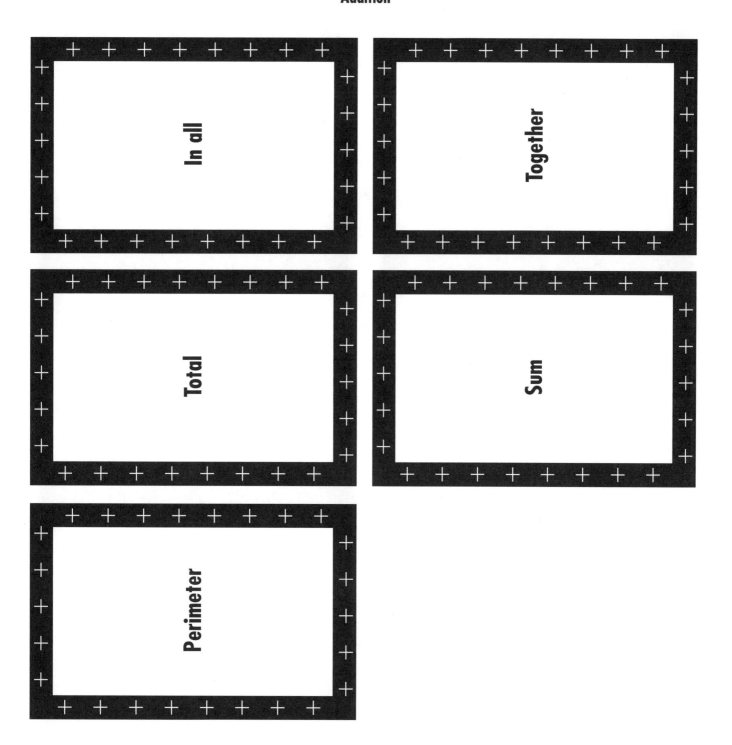

In all

Together

Total

Sum

Perimeter

Idea 7

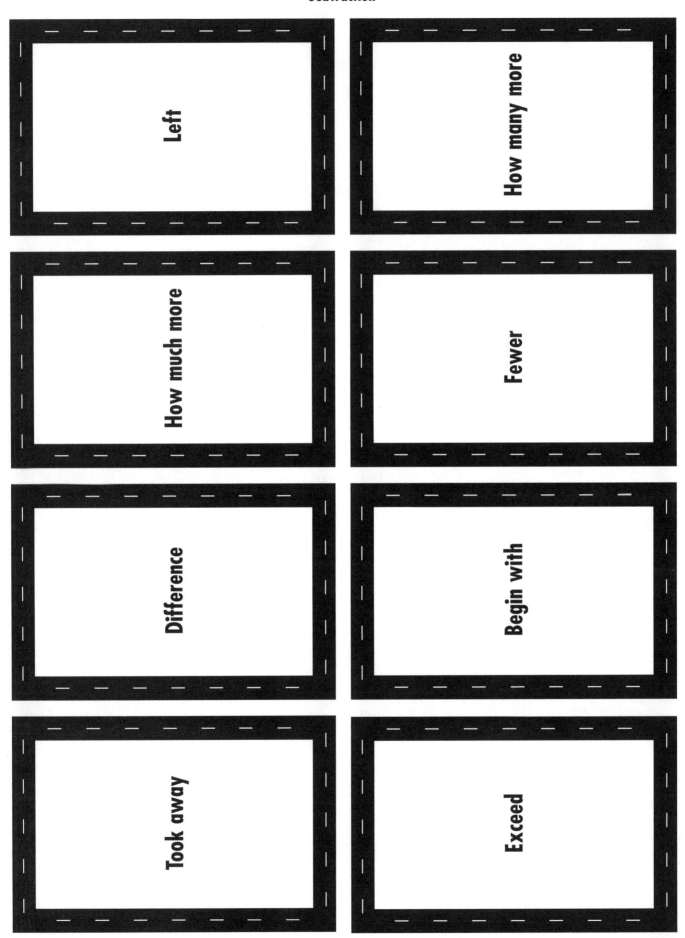

Left

How many more

How much more

Fewer

Difference

Begin with

Took away

Exceed

40

Idea 7

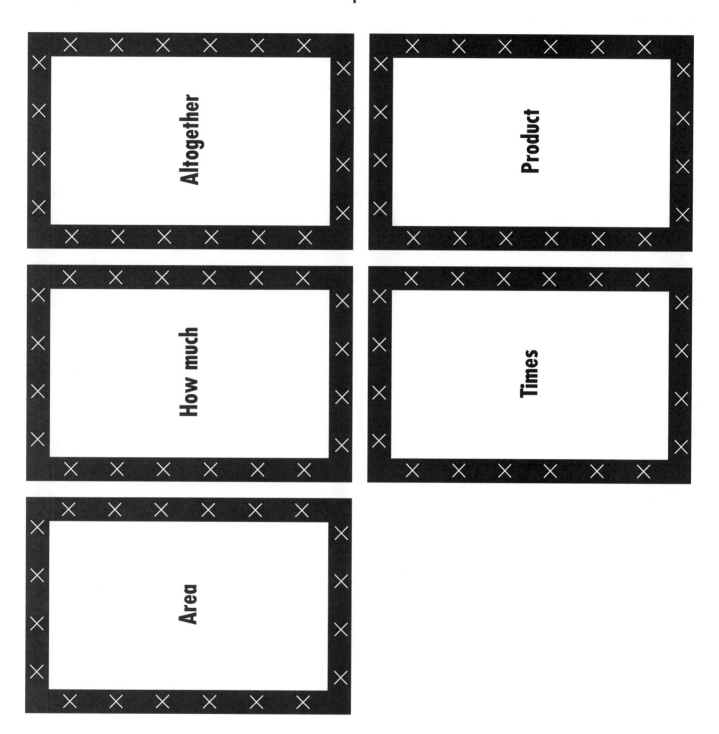

Idea 7

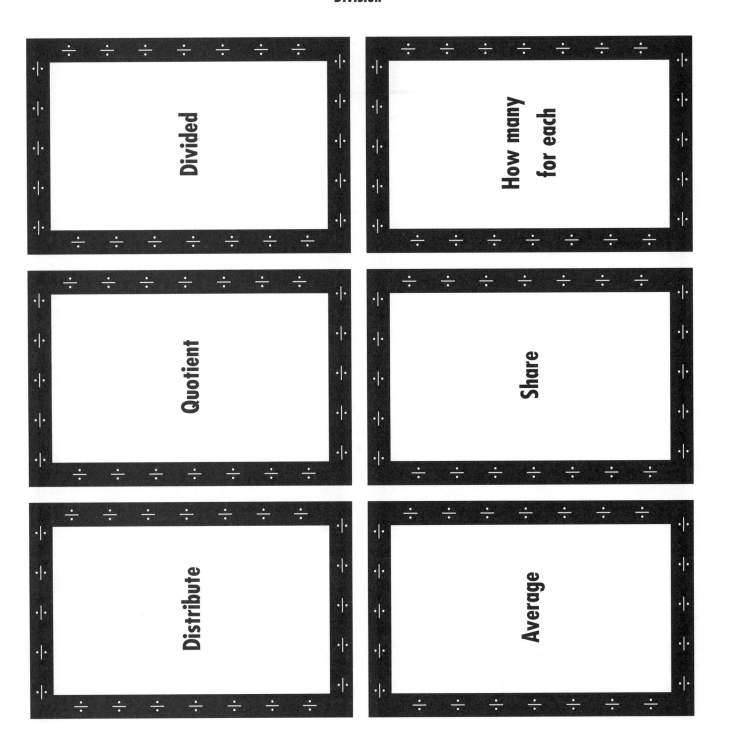

Divided

How many for each

Quotient

Share

Distribute

Average

42

43

Addition

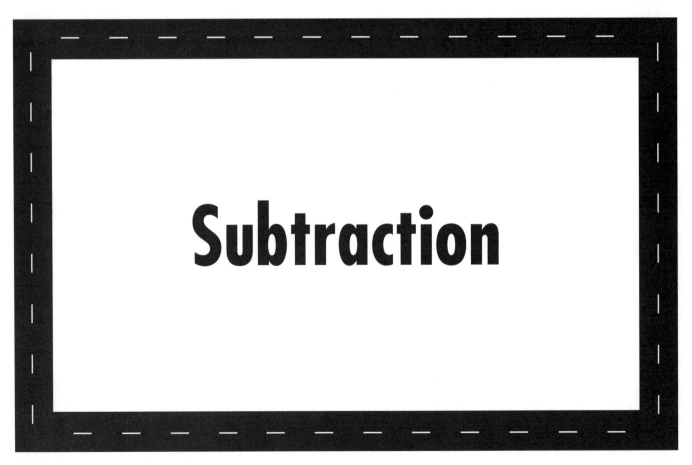

Subtraction

Multiplication

Division

Operation Word Clues

Addition

In All
Together
Total
Sum
Perimeter

_____
_____
_____

Subtraction

Left   Difference
How many more   Begin with
How much more   Took Away
Fewer   Exceed

_____
_____
_____

Multiplication

Altogether
Product
How much
Times
Area

_____
_____
_____

Division

Divided
How many for each
Quotient
Share
Distribute
Average

_____
_____
_____

Idea 7

Idea 8
Parts Are Parts

Teaching students about prefixes and suffixes helps them expand their vocabulary. Explicitly teaching students about word parts, which include prefixes, suffixes, and root words, is an important strategy to help them expand their vocabulary by using words they already know to help them understand new words they encounter while reading. Begin with the most commonly used prefixes and suffixes from the list we have provided.

Here are some ways to help students begin to build this knowledge.

Direct Teach

❶ Introduce students to a few prefixes or suffixes at a time. Tell them the meaning of each affix you introduce.

❷ Share a root word that students already know. Place a prefix that will make a new word, and read the new word for the students (e.g., *un–* in front of the word *aware* to form the new word *unaware*).

❸ Ask students to define the new word and use it in a sentence.

❹ Continue to present examples, using both prefixes and suffixes, until students understand how to decompose a word containing affixes into parts.

Card Games

❶ Fill out the blank cards with root words that go along with the text reading. Have students play a card game using the suffix, prefix, and root word cards, provided, using a *Memory* format. Place the cards facedown between two students. Player 1 turns over two cards. If the cards match (a match is an affix and root word that can be combined to form a new word) and player 1 identifies it as a match, he or she takes the two cards and another turn. If the cards do not match, it is player 2's turn.

❷ Small groups of students may work with a deck containing only prefix and/or suffix cards. They can take turns drawing a card and then try to create a new word by combining it with a list of root words provided by the teacher.

❸ Have students use a *Go Fish* format in which the deck includes prefixes, suffixes, and root words (created using the blank cards, provided). A group of four students divides the deck of cards. Player 1 begins asking another player to name one prefix, suffix, or root word in his or her hand. After the student states the affix or root word, player 1 says, "I have a root word that can be used with your suffix to form a new word." Examples include: "I have the root word *available* that will go with your prefix *un–* to form the new word *unavailable*," or "I have the suffix *–able* that will go with your root word *understand* to form the new word *understandable*." If the student can correctly form a new word, he or she gets the pair, and player 2 takes a turn.

Prereading Activity

Choose vocabulary words that contain prefixes or suffixes from content-area textbooks before students begin reading the text. Provide the word list to students (use the form provided), and ask them to work in pairs to try to guess the meaning of the word, based on their knowledge of the affix and the root word.

Prereading Activity

Text and Chapter _Earth and Science Systems, Chapter 7_

New Vocabulary Words	What do you think these words mean?
In-dependent	
Bi-ology	
Ge-ology	
Steep-ness	
Sub-strata	
Re-current	
Dia-gram	

Frequently Used Prefixes and Suffixes

Prefix	Meaning	Suffix	Meaning
un-	Not, opposite of	-able	Inclined to
re-	Again	-er	One who
il-, ir-	Not	-est	Most
dis-	Not, opposite of	-ful	Full of
en-, em-	Cause to	-gram	Written
non-	Not	-ly	Every
in-, im-	Not	-less	Without
over-	Too much	-ment	Action or process
mis-	Wrongly	-ness	State of being
sub-	Under	-ology	Study of
pre-	Before		
inter-	Between		
fore-	Before		

Prereading Activity

Text and Chapter _____

New Vocabulary Words   **What do you think these words mean?**

_____   _____

_____   _____

_____   _____

_____   _____

_____   _____

_____   _____

_____   _____

_____   _____

_____   _____

_____   _____

_____

Idea 8

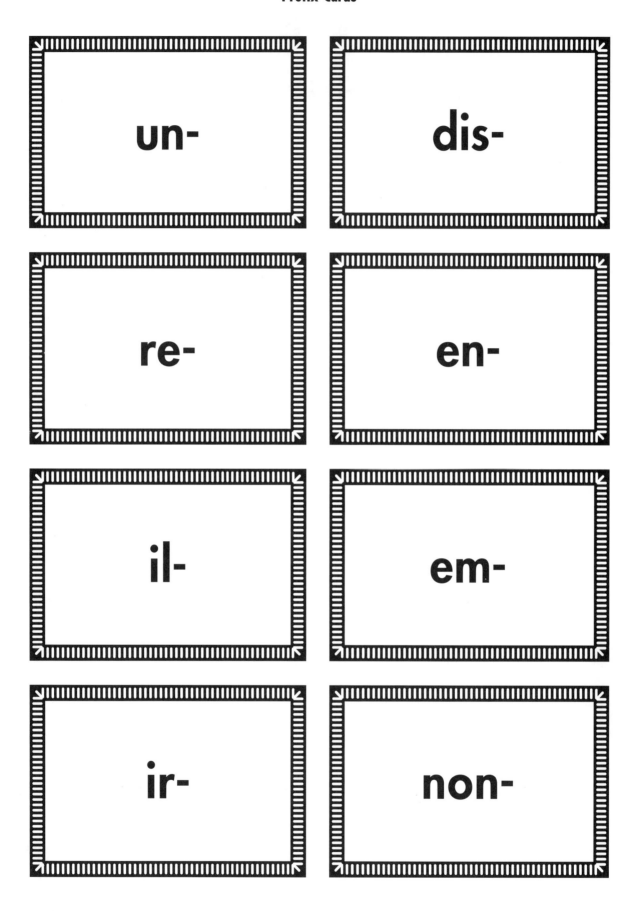

un-

dis-

re-

en-

il-

em-

ir-

non-

50

Idea 8

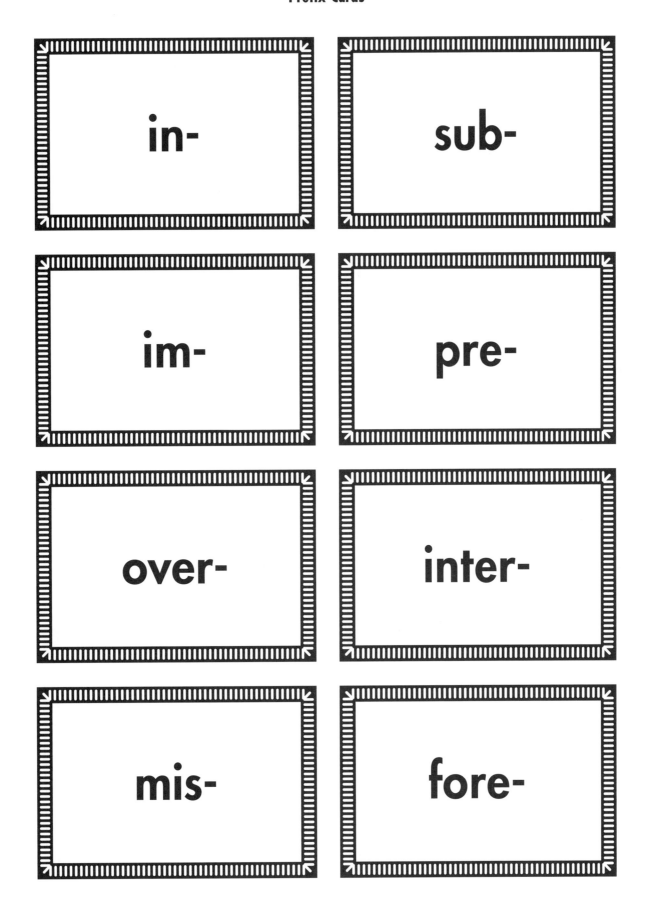

in-

sub-

im-

pre-

over-

inter-

mis-

fore-

51

Idea 8

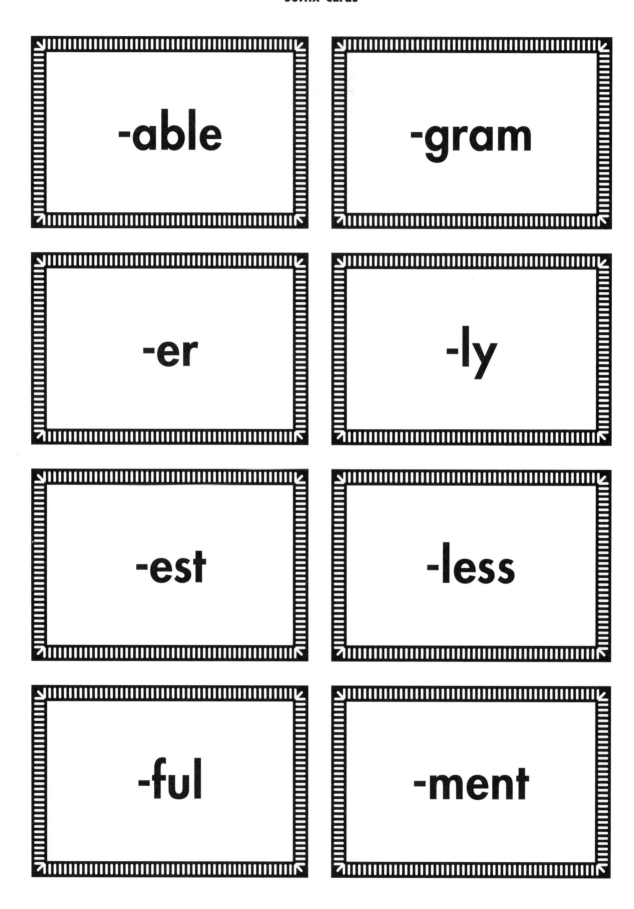

-able

-gram

-er

-ly

-est

-less

-ful

-ment

Idea 8

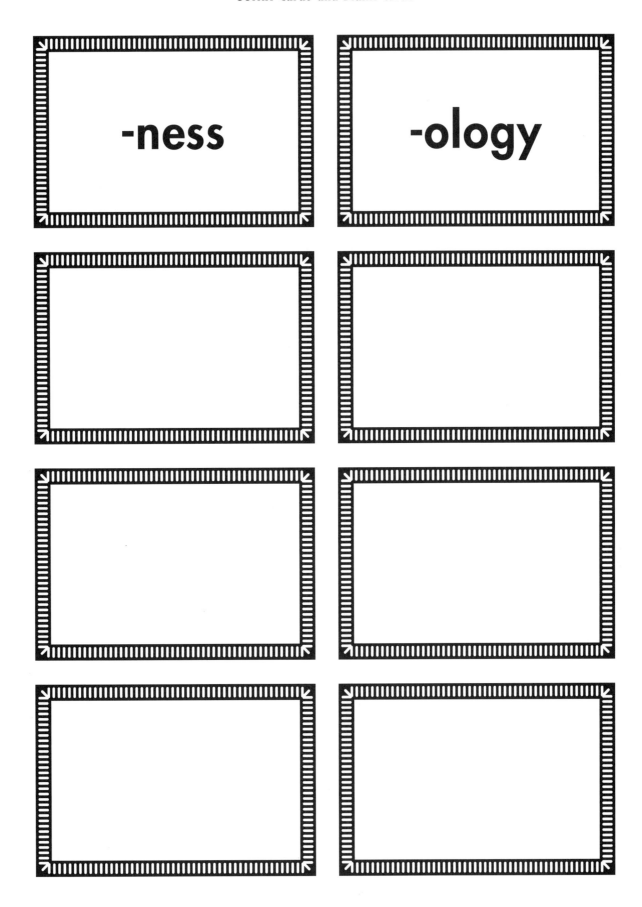

-ness

-ology

53

Idea 8

Idea 9
Visual Definition

Schwartz and Raphael's 1985 "concept of definition" is a great example of a simple but effective vocabulary tool that teachers have found useful for many years. The concept-of-definition map is a graphic organizer that can be used to introduce students to new vocabulary and help them remember it. Using this type of tool encourages students to link their own knowledge to a new concept.

Because of the wealth of research supporting the use of visuals to improve memory and comprehension, we have modified the original graphic design to include a visual representation of the word. However, we suggest using the original questions from Schwartz and Raphael to help students understand the full definition of a new vocabulary word:

- What is it? (Category)
- What are some examples or illustrations?
- What is it like? (Attributes)

Introduce the Visual Definition chart with a vocabulary word that students already know. Demonstrate how to complete the chart, step by step, displaying each step with a document projector, whiteboard, or chart tablet.

Here is an example.

❶ Start with the word *affix*, which you would write in the Vocabulary Word box in the center of the chart.

❷ Ask students the first question, "What is it?" They might say, "Something you add to a base or root word," which would be a correct category and general enough for all students to understand.

❸ Ask students to give examples. They might say, "unbelievable" or "disagreement." In addition, ask students to draw a picture.

Note. This idea is from *Practical Ideas That Really Work for Secondary Students in Inclusive Classrooms* (pp. 41–45), by K. McConnell and G. R. Ryser, 2007, Austin, TX: PRO-ED, Inc. Copyright 2007 by PRO-ED, Inc. Reprinted with permission. The original idea is based on "Concept of Definition: A Key to Improving Students' Vocabulary," by R. M. Schwartz and T. E. Raphael, 1985, *The Reading Teacher, 39,* pp. 190–205. Copyright 1985 by Intenational Reading Association.

④ Ask "What is it like?" to give students a chance to list the attributes. They could name a number of characteristics, including "Add to the beginning," "Add to the end," "Changes the meaning," and "Prefix or suffix."

⑤ After completing the Visual Definition, ask students to look at their papers and tell the definition of *affix,* either to you or to a partner. A good definition might be, "An affix is one or more letters added to the beginning or ending of a root word that changes the meaning of the word."

Students should learn from this example that the visual definition not only provides a thorough explanation of the word, it also allows them to add their own individual knowledge and background. The addition of the visual should help them remember the meaning of the word. After modeling with an example, repeat this process with a vocabulary word from the students' content material.

Not all students will at first be able to complete the Visual Definition on their own, so encourage them to work in teams of two or three, and then have some students share their definitions with the whole class. When checking students for mastery, cover up the word with a small piece of paper, show them the rest of the map, and see if they can guess the word. Students can also self-check this way.

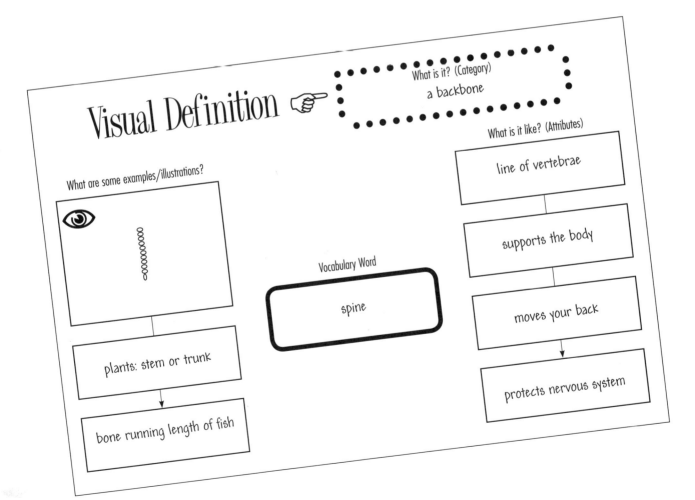

Visual Definition

☞

What is it? (Category)

What is it like? (Attributes)

Vocabulary Word

What are some examples/illustrations?

Visual Definition 👉

What is it? (Category)

What are some examples/illustrations?

What is it like? (Attributes)

Vocabulary Word

Visual Definition 👉

What is it? (Category)

What are some examples/illustrations?

What is it like? (Attributes)

Vocabulary Word

Idea 9

Idea 10
Vocabulary Puzzles

One reason students have difficulty comprehending content-area material is that they lack sufficient background knowledge of the subject. Sometimes they are not even familiar with the common vocabulary related to the subject. When students lack such basic familiarity, asking them to look up and copy definitions from the dictionary is often meaningless and ineffective. Strategies for teaching new vocabulary will be more effective if students are encouraged to construct their own definitions. Vocabulary Puzzles are a great way to help students construct definitions and can also be wonderful tools for independent study. The puzzles are paper strips that include the vocabulary word, a visual cue to the word's meaning, and a definition written in the student's own words.

Here's how to create the puzzles.

❶ Cut tagboard or stiff paper into strips measuring about 2 in. by 8 in.

❷ Give students a list of vocabulary terms that will be found in a targeted reading.

❸ Have students work together in pairs to find each term in the text and to read the section of text in which the new word is used.

❹ Students decide on a sentence or phrase that defines and/or explains the term. They also decide on a picture that illustrates the term.

❺ Students then create the puzzle by drawing the picture on the first third of the strip, writing the word on the second third, and writing the definition on the last third. Cut along the puzzle lines that divide the puzzle to cut apart.

Ways to Use Vocabulary Puzzles

• Students can work alone or with their partner to put the pieces of the puzzles together as they work on learning the meaning of new vocabulary.

• A pair of students can challenge another pair to complete each other's puzzles. This works well if the pairs have created puzzles for different sets of words. Students may be challenged to explain how they decided on a definition or a picture cue.

• Have students develop the puzzles prior to reading all of the text. This sets a purpose for reading and prepares students to better understand the material.

Tips:

⊙ To increase the level of difficulty, use the same puzzle pattern for several words.

⊙ Write an answer key (e.g., 1, 2, 3 or a, b, c) on the back of the puzzle pieces so that students can use them for a review activity prior to a chapter test. The same puzzles (without the keys on back) can be used for the test.

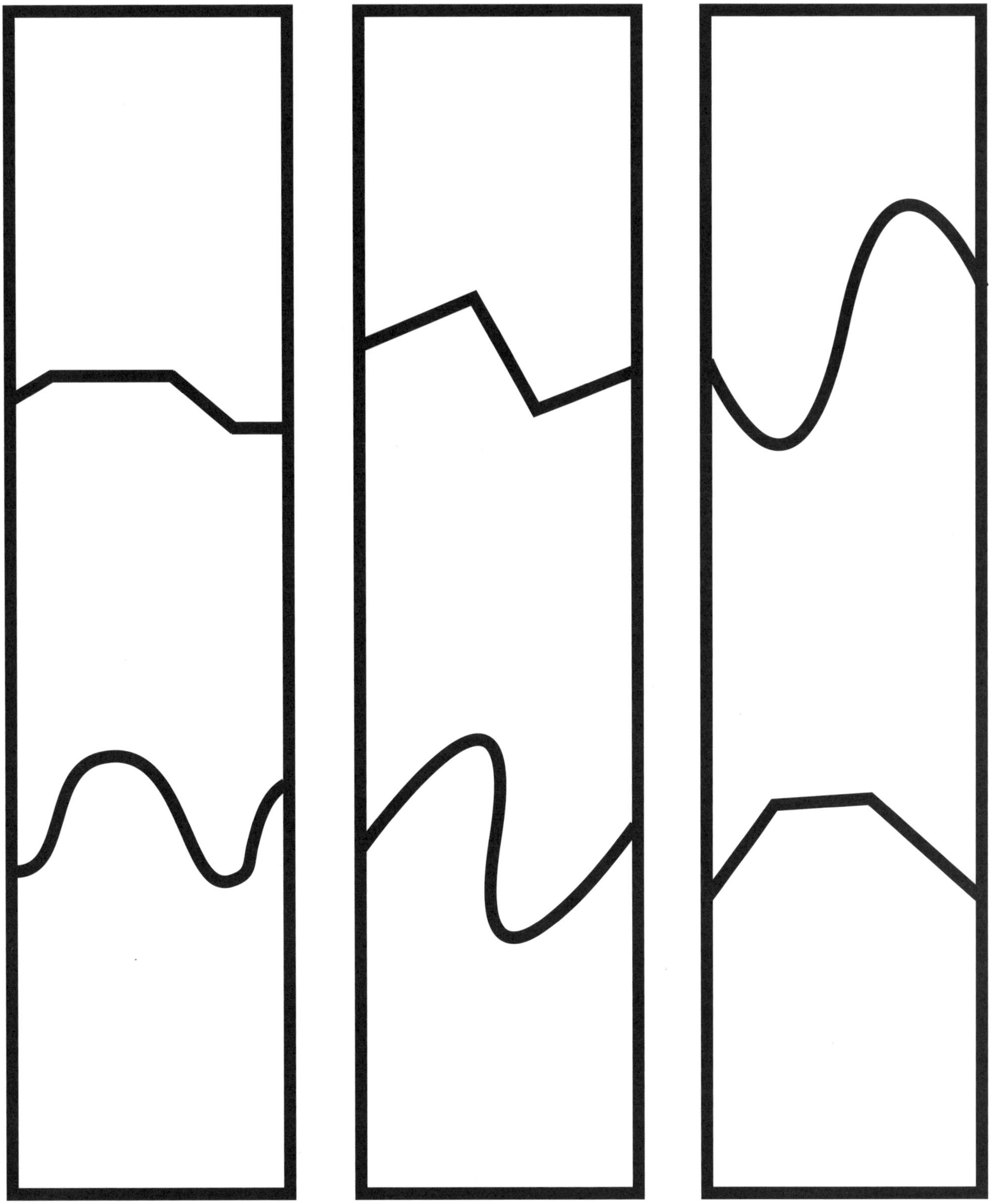

Idea 11
Dictionary Games

To help all students become independent, lifelong learners, basic dictionary skills should be taught at an early age, not just for dictionary use, but also for competence with a glossary and a thesaurus. Students who are proficient in dictionary use will know how to get help for spelling, pronunciation, definitions, synonyms and antonyms, usage, syllabication, parts of speech, and the origin or history of words.

Sequential lists of dictionary skills can be found in reading and writing curricula as well on many Internet Web sites. In addition to teaching basic dictionary skills, the following activities and games can be used with students of almost any age to provide practice and to make learning dictionary skills fun.

Word of the Day

This is a great warm-up activity for the beginning of class.

- Assign students to two-person teams, and give each team a noisemaker.
- Select 10 to 15 words that are relevant, not just to your subject but to all core subjects, and write one word on the board.
- Ask students to work with a partner for a maximum of 2 minutes to find the word in the dictionary, tell the definition in their own words, and use it correctly in a meaningful sentence.
- Set the timer and wait for a team to signal first. Give the first team that signals an opportunity to respond correctly. If they do, they earn a point; if not, call on the next team.
- The team with the most points can pick a prize coupon. We have provided four, along with some blank coupons for you to make up your own.

Word of the Day—Simplified

This activity is just like the Word of the Day, except with a simpler goal. For students who are still struggling with using the dictionary, vary the activity by calling out or writing a word. However, all the students must do is tell you the number of the page the word is on and the entry or guide words at the top of that page.

✗ Tip:

There are many Internet resources for teaching or learning dictionary skills. While we do not endorse any specific Internet content, the Web site www.dictionary.com has a wide range of resources and links to other sites.

Name That Word

- The teacher calls out or writes a page number from the dictionary and a part of speech.

- Students, either individually or in pairs, must find a word on the page that is an example of the part of speech named.

- Once students find the word, they must tell its meaning.

- Award points and prizes.

Name That Word—Bumped Up

For this practice activity, the teacher follows the same procedure as in Name That Word, except using very specific types of words (e.g., words with prefixes, words with suffixes, or plurals).

Five Chances, Four Chances, Three Chances

This game is intended to help students who are having difficulty with alphabetical order or with guide words. For this activity, students need a bookmark and a dictionary.

- The teacher calls out a word, and students try to find the page the word is on as quickly as possible. (To do so, students should already know which initial letters are found in which part of the dictionary. For example, words that start with *b* are in the first quarter; words that start with *w* are in the last quarter.)

- After the teacher calls out or writes a word, students open their dictionaries the first time and put their bookmarks on the page they selected. (Students might get lucky and open to the correct page on the first try, but it does not happen very often.)

- Students then close the dictionary, leaving their bookmarks sticking out of the dictionary.

- The teacher says the word again, and students open their dictionaries for the second time, knowing that they must open it either before or after their first try.

- Students should move their book marks to the new page and then close their dictionaries.

- Repeat this activity until all students have found the correct page, beginning with five chances, then four, and then finally three chances for students who are getting very proficient.

- Provide extra instruction and practice for students who can't find the correct page after five attempts.

What's the Word?

- This is a good activity for two or three teams, each of which works together and has a section of the board on which to write their answers.

- The teacher writes two guide words at the top of the board.

- Under the guide words, the teacher writes a definition of a word that is on the page with these two guide words.

- When the teacher gives a signal, students must quickly find the word defined by the teacher and write it on the board.

- The first team to write the correct word scores a point.

- Repeat this 10 times, and give the winning team a reward.

No Homework

Late One Day

Leave Early for Lunch

Three Extra Points on a Quiz

Idea 11

Idea 12
Three Clues

Students can use the Three Clues strategy to create a fun game to use when reviewing for a test. Write a different vocabulary word on Side One of each card. Divide the class into groups of three or four students and pass out the cards. Ask students to write three clues on Side Two of the card. The clues should be general at first (number 3), then gradually more specific (number 1). After students complete their clues, have the first group read their clues one at a time, from 3 to 1, pausing after each clue. The group who guesses the word first gets a point and reads their first clue. When all the words are finished, place the cards in a center for students to study individually.

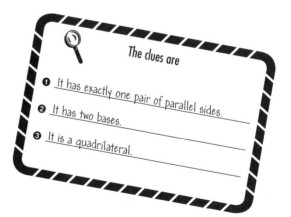

Three Clues

The word is

_____

Three Clues

The word is

_____

Three Clues

The word is

_____

Idea 12

The clues are

1 _____

2 _____

3 _____

The clues are

1 _____

2 _____

3 _____

The clues are

1 _____

2 _____

3 _____

Idea 12

Idea 13

Graphic Organizers: Vocabulary Development

Graphic organizers help students develop and improve their vocabulary, and students can use them individually, with partners, or in a group. In this idea, we have provided two graphic organizers that can be used to develop vocabulary in all content areas.

Follow these steps.

1. Project the blank graphic organizer.

2. Explain how it is used by completing the form.

3. Show the students several completed examples.

4. Check students' progress when they first begin using the form.

5. Ask students to share their completed graphic organizers with the rest of the class.

Getting Used to It

How well do I know the word?

New Vocabulary	I have never heard of it.	I have heard of it but don't know what it means	I have some idea of what it means.	I know what it means but don't use it.	I am used to it. I use it, and here is what it means:
1 petiole 10-3	10-3		10-6		10-9 A petiole is the part of the leaf that attaches it to the plant.
2 node 10-3		10-3		10-5	10-6 The part of a stem that normally bears a leaf is called the node.
3 epidermis 10-3			10-3		10-4 The epidermis is a thin layer of cells that form the outer coating of the plant.
4					
5					
6					

71

Instructions

Getting Used to It

The Getting Used to It form shows the steps that all people go through every time they learn a new word. To use the form, identify new vocabulary words at the beginning of a topic of study. Tell students to write the words they don't know in the New Vocabulary box in the first column, and note the starting date underneath the word. Have students place the form in the front of their notebook or another place for safekeeping. As instruction continues, students should note the date in the next four columns as they reach each step. When students feel that they have made the word their own, have them write the date in the last column, along with the word's definition, and have them give an example of when they have used the word.

Table It

Use the Table It form to organize key vocabulary words in a unit of study. Students write three to five key vocabulary words across the top row, the page number(s) of the text on which the word appears in the second row, a sentence using the word in the third row, and a synonym in the fourth row.

Getting Used to It

How well do I know the word?

New Vocabulary	I have never heard of it.	I have heard of it but don't know what it means.	I have some idea of what it means.	I know what it means but don't use it.	I am used to it. I use it, and here is what it means:
❶					
❷					
❸					
❹					
❺					
❻					

73

Idea 13

Table It

✕ ◎ ◎ ✕			
Page Numbers	_____	_____	_____
Sentence			
Synonym			

74

Table It

⟲✗				
Page Numbers				
Sentence				
Synonym				

Idea 14
REACH

You can improve students' reading comprehension by teaching them how to preview a topic. The main purposes of preview strategies are to

• Help students think about what they already know about the topic

• Get students interested in finding out about the topic

• Assist students in making predictions about the topic

Teach students the REACH mnemonic. Before reading a text, have students spend 5 minutes to REACH.

Here is the REACH mnemonic.

R Read the title.

E Examine the pictures, tables, and diagrams.

A Ask yourself what the section headings mean.

C Canvass for key words (bold, underlined, italics).

H Highlight the important parts of the first and last paragraphs.

Note. This idea is based on "K-W-L: A Teaching Model That Develops Active Reading of Expository Text," by D. M. Ogle, 1986, *The Reading Teacher, 39,* pp. 564–570. Copyright 1986 by International Reading Association.

REACH

R ead the title. ☐

E xamine the pictures, tables, and diagrams. ☐

A sk yourself what the section headings mean. ☐

C anvass for key words (bold, underlined, italics). ☐

H ighlight important parts of the first and last paragraphs. ☐

REACH

R ead the title.   ☐

E xamine the pictures, tables, and diagrams.   ☐

A sk yourself what the section headings mean.   ☐

C anvass for key words (bold, underlined, italics).   ☐

H ighlight important parts of the first and last paragraphs.   ☐

REACH

R ead the title.   ☐

E xamine the pictures, tables, and diagrams.   ☐

A sk yourself what the section headings mean.   ☐

C anvass for key words (bold, underlined, italics).   ☐

H ighlight important parts of the first and last paragraphs.   ☐

Idea 14

Idea 15
Highlighting

Highlighting is a widely used accommodation for students who have limited reading skills. Teachers can highlight the important information in a text to help students focus on main ideas and to reduce the reading load of content-area courses. Take this modification a step further and teach students to do their own highlighting. This strategy will benefit every student in the classroom.

Here is how to get started.

❶ Give all students a photocopy of a text selection.

❷ Explain the benefits of highlighting:
- Focuses on only the important information in the text
- Good study skill because it easily shows what's important in the chapter

❸ Teach each aspect of highlighting as a separate skill. See the What to Highlight section on the next page.

❹ Model through use of an overhead projector and whole-group discussion.

❺ Put students into groups of two or three and have them decide what needs to be highlighted.

🕷 Tip:

Many office or school supply stores now sell highlighting tape. All students have to do is peel off a length of tape and cover the line of text they want to highlight. When they are finished studying, the tape can be erased with a pencil eraser.

What to Highlight

☆ Answers to end-of-chapter questions

☆ Vocabulary words and their definitions

☆ Answers to worksheet questions

☆ Key words on study guides

☆ Explanations of figures

How to Use Color Coding

❀ Use yellow for answers to questions

❀ Use blue for vocabulary words

❀ Use pink for definitions of vocabulary words

❀ Use green for references to figures

Idea 16
Get Graphic

Important quantitative data are often presented in tables, figures, diagrams, and other graphically oriented formats, and students must be able to interpret relevant information from these formats. This idea assists students in pulling relevant information from any type of graphically oriented format. We have provided two forms: Describe the Graphic is used when you want students to pull out the literal information, and Interpret the Graphic is used when you want students to analyze the information.

Here's how it works.

❶ Direct students to examine the table, figure, diagram, or other graphic-oriented material.

❷ Teach students how to use Describe the Graphic by giving each student a copy of the form and following the directions.

❸ After students understand how Describe the Graphic works, teach them how to use Interpret the Graphic by giving each student a copy of the form and following the directions.

❹ Model how to complete the forms.
  ⊙ Write the title and page number of the graphic on the first line.
  ⊙ Circle the format of the graphic.

Describe the Graphic
⊙ Ask students to identify the key labels used in the graphic and write them under the heading *Label*.
⊙ Record what each label represents next to it (e.g., name, probability).
⊙ Write one fact about the graph.

Interpret the Graphic
  ⊙ Write questions about the graph in the *Questions* column. The teacher can write these ahead of time or ask students to write their own.
  ⊙ Have students answer each question in the *Answers* column.

 Tip:

For homework, have students find a graph from a newspaper or news magazine and complete the two forms.

Note. This idea is from *Practical Ideas That Really Work for Teaching Math Problem Solving* (pp. 93–95), by G. R. Ryser, J. R. Patton, E. A. Polloway, and K. McConnell, 2006, Austin, TX: PRO-ED, Inc. Copyright 2006 by PRO-ED, Inc. Reprinted with permission.

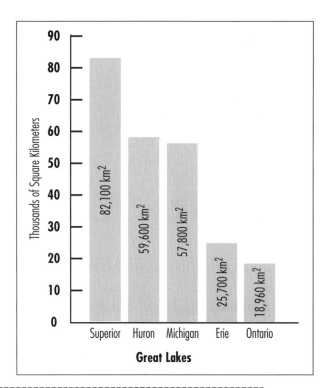

Great Lakes

Describe the Graphic

Title of Graphic: _Great Lakes_   Page: _56_

Format: table   graph   diagram   (other)

Label	What It Represents
• _Great Lakes_	• _names of the five Great Lakes_
• _Square KM_	• _surface area in square km of each Great Lake_
• _____	• _____

Write one fact about the graph.

Lake Superior is the largest.

Interpret the Graphic

Title of Graphic: _Great Lakes_   Page: _56_

Format: table   graph   diagram   (other)

Questions	Answers
• _Would it take longer to go around Lake Superior or Lake Michigan?_	• _Lake Superior_
• _Which lake is the smallest?_	• _Lake Ontario_
• _Which two lakes are about the same size?_	• _Lake Huron and Lake Michigan_
• _____	• _____

Idea 16

Describe the Graphic

Title of Graphic: _____ Page: _____

Format: table   graph   diagram   other

Label | **What It Represents**

- _____ • _____
- _____ • _____
- _____ • _____

Write one fact about the graph.

Interpret the Graphic

Title of Graphic: _____ Page: _____

Format: table   graph   diagram   other

Questions | **Answers**

- _____ • _____
  _____   _____
- _____ • _____
  _____   _____
- _____ • _____
  _____   _____
- _____ • _____

Idea 16

Idea 17
Figure It Out

Not all important information in a reading passage can be found in paragraphs. When students are reading content-area text, they need to know how to understand information presented graphically (e.g., tables, figures, diagrams, maps). Some students read carefully enough to comprehend the meaning of what is presented in graphic formats, but others will require teacher instruction and practice.

Model the steps with visual examples, checking often for understanding. Demonstrate the steps while speaking out loud, so that students can hear your explanation. This "think aloud" strategy will help students who need help with the process. After completing each step, give students some practice text and ask them questions, either verbally, in writing, or both.

Here are the key steps.

❶ Read the title of the table, figure, diagram, or map. Highlight it. Define the key terms in the title. In our example, the table title is "Ideology and Age." Students should highlight the title as you explain the meaning of *ideology* and clarify that the table considers two variables, ideology and age. Check for understanding with random questioning.

❷ If there is a source for the graphic, it will usually be shown at the bottom of the graphic, often in small print. Point it out to your students and read it aloud. In our example, the source is a 2003 Gallup Poll. The teacher would make sure students understand what a "poll" is and explain the nature of the Gallup Organization's polling.

❸ Read the headings and other key words, which are often in large, capital, or bold-face type. If a map is being reviewed, read the legend. Highlight the headings in a second color. In the example, you would first read the two key questions that were the basis for participants' responses. You would also point out the bold terms *Age, Conservative, Moderate,* and *Liberal,* explaining that these are the categories of ideology most people refer to when they describe themselves or others in political terms. Again, check for understanding, making sure all students understand.

❹ Ask questions based on the table, starting first with *right there* questions, meaning the answers are right there, and no inferences or conclusions need to be drawn. Questions of this type in our example would begin with "What percent . . ." "What age group . . ." "Which ideology . . ." These factual questions could also ask for comparisons (using words like *greater than* or *less than*). Ask each student at least one of these basic questions.

❺ The last step is to ask students questions that call for conclusions, inferences, and assumptions (*look for it* or *think about it* questions). These questions are more difficult but are often found on standardized tests. An example might be, "Do people get more conservative or more liberal on economic issues as they get older?" This type of question can be answered with the information provided, but students may need to hear you model the thinking process that is required to arrive at a correct answer. Again, modeling the "think aloud" steps is essential for some students.

❻ After completing this instructional sequence, review (either by asking students questions you have already written or by asking students to write four questions each) two that can be answered directly from the information provided and two that require deeper thinking. Collect all of their questions and use them for the review.

Table 4.1
Ideology and Age

Thinking about social issues, would you say your views on social issues are conservative, moderate, or liberal?

Age	Conservative	Moderate	Liberal
18–24	27%	36%	36%
25–38	33%	34%	31%
39 plus	40%	38%	19%

Thinking about economic issues, would you say your views on economic issues are conservative, moderate, or liberal?

Age	Conservative	Moderate	Liberal
18–24	33%	40%	26%
25–38	39%	39%	20%
39 plus	47%	38%	12%

Source: Gallup Poll reported May 20, 2003. Copyright © 2003 by The Gallup Organization.

Idea 18

Think Out Loud

Students must process information from text to succeed in school. Think Out Loud is a strategy that helps students construct explanations of text as they read. We have provided bookmarks that you can copy on card stock and give to your students to remind them of the strategies to use for Think Out Loud: one for English/Social Studies and one for Mathematics/Science. These bookmarks have two blank lines on which students can write additional strategies, and there is also a blank bookmark that teachers can use to implement their own strategies.

Here is how Think Out Loud works.

❶ Begin with a short section of text (one or two pages) to model the strategy.

❷ Discuss with your students different strategies to use as they "think out loud." Sample strategies include Visualize, Make Predictions, Identify a Problem, Ask Questions, Make Comparisons, and Determine Cause and Effect.

❸ Provide students with a purpose for the reading.

❹ Read the text and model the chosen strategies as you read by stopping often to "think out loud" about what you have just read.

❺ Ask students to annotate the text as you read by underlining the words that triggered the use of the strategies you are modeling. For example, if you are modeling Make Predictions, students should underline or circle the words that provide clues about what will happen next.

❻ After you finish modeling, have students work in pairs to think out loud. As they read, ask them to identify additional strategies that they used.

English/Social Studies

Visualize

Make Predictions

Make Comparisons

Determine Cause and Effect

_____

_____

Mathematics/Science

Visualize

Identify a Problem

Ask Questions

Make Predictions

_____

_____

_____

_____

_____

_____

_____

_____

_____

Idea 18

Idea 19
Got It Gallery

Visualizing while reading really does improve comprehension, so helping students master the strategy is important. This idea provides a framework to help students visualize as they read. Because mastering the strategy may be challenging to some students, it might be necessary to repeat these steps with several reading passages, keeping in mind that learning the strategy is as important as learning specific content. If students are unfamiliar with the content, make sure that you have used some prereading strategies, like those presented in Idea 14, REACH, Idea 15, Highlighting, and the first section of Idea 28, Look Ahead and Look Back.

Here is how the Got It Gallery works.

❶ Select a reading passage and divide it into three to five sections. Prepare students for understanding by reviewing the title, illustrations, and key headings of the passage.

❷ Explain to students that they will be reading and illustrating sections of a reading passage, and that by illustrating the content they read and then visualizing their illustrations, they will "get it," more easily.

❸ Ask students to read the first section. Sometimes you will want them to read orally and sometimes silently, depending on the content and purpose.

❹ Ask some brief questions to determine students' understanding, and cue them if they are confused or unsure of the first section's meaning. Once you are sure that students understand what they just read, ask each student to draw a picture that represents the first section's content or action. This drawing should go in the first frame of their Got It Gallery. Limit the time allowed for the drawing by using a timer set for about 3 minutes, so that students do not get bogged down in their illustrations and forget the content of the passage.

❺ After the first drawing is in the gallery, tell students to close their eyes and think about their illustration. Ask them to pretend they are looking at the picture in the frame. Then tell them to whisper what they see to themselves. Move around the room, and quietly ask one or two students to tell you what they see in their first frame.

🌀 Tips:

⊙ During this process, ask one or more students to model by completing large illustrations on individual sheets of paper. The illustrations should be posted from left to right on a bulletin board or an empty wall as the class reads each section of the passage.

⊙ There are many software packages and online clip-art files available, so teachers should have no problem presenting a variety of styles to fit the content of students' reading.

❻ After reviewing their first frame (and the content in the first section of text they read), tell students to open their eyes, read the next section of their passage, and complete the second illustration in their gallery. Repeat this process until each student has read and illustrated the three to five sections, completing the entire passage.

❼ When reading and drawing are completed, students should review the events, actions, or content that they read about and illustrated. Tell students to use the pictures as a tool to master the content.

❽ After a quick review, ask students to close their eyes and try to remember the first picture they drew, then the second, then the third, and so on. With their eyes still closed, ask individual students to recount the content of their reading. Continue the questioning and visual descriptions until all students have contributed.

❾ Instruct students to review their gallery often, closing their eyes and visualizing until they've "got it." Emphasize that visualization is a study strategy that can be used often, with few materials and in almost any situation. For students who do not have an adult helping them study at home, visualization can help them until they've got it on their own.

Got It Gallery ___ of a Butterfly ___

Egg

Larva ➔ Caterpillar

Caterpillar

Pupa ➔ Chrysalis

Adult ➔ Butterfly

Got It Gallery

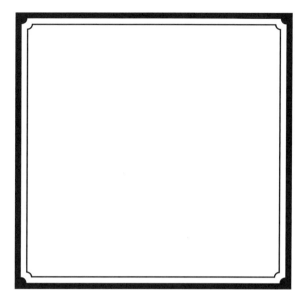

93

Idea 19

Got It Gallery

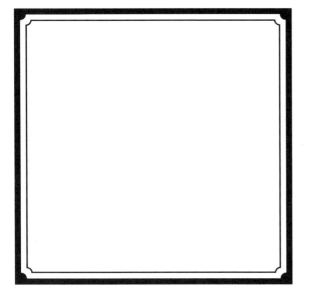

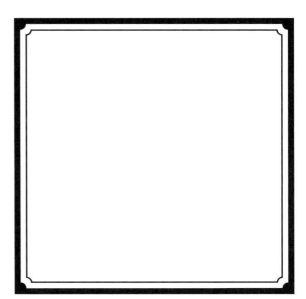

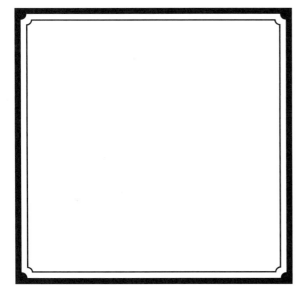

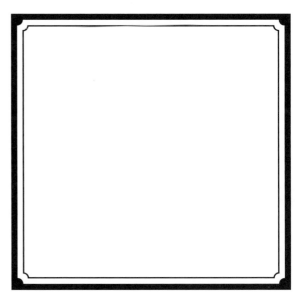

Idea 19

Got It Gallery

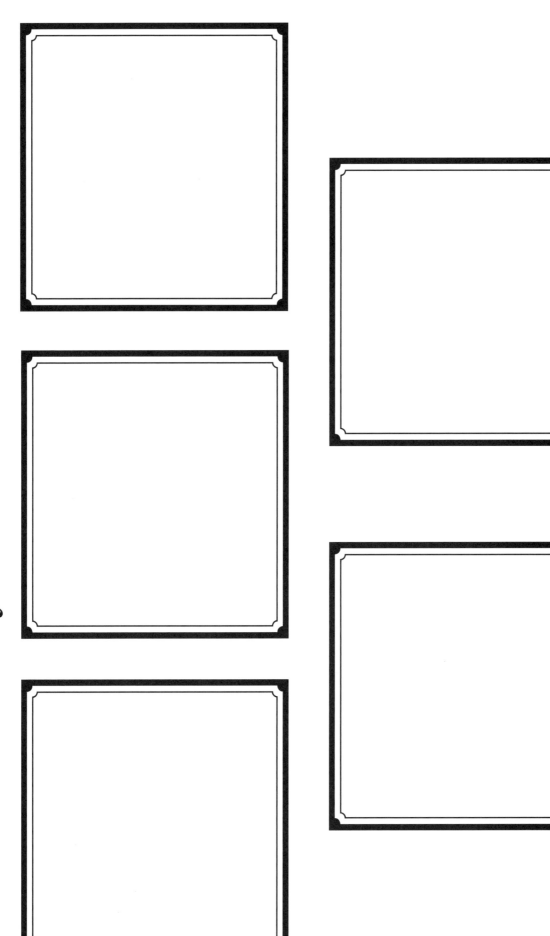

Idea 20
Make-and-Take Study Helpers

When students have difficulty with vocabulary, comprehension, and meta-cognitive skills, it is important that teachers give them the tools they need to study and practice independently. Fortunately, there are many study tools that can be used by students in school as well as at home. We have provided two related ideas for hands-on study helpers, both of which are quick and easy to make. The first one, Two-Part Folded Graphic, is useful for two-step procedures, cause-and-effect relationships, or two facts about the same topic. The second one, Five-Part Folded Graphic, is useful for vocabulary words and for multiple-step sequences, like events in a work of fiction, steps in a science experiment, sequential steps for completing a math problem, or events during a significant period in history. Any content can be studied with these tools—words and definitions, math facts or steps in a problem, concepts and examples, cause and effect, visual representations of definitions or key words, synonyms and antonyms, summaries of events, sequence of actions, character traits of historical figures—the possibilities are numerous and diverse.

Two-Part Folded Graphic

❶ Fold a sheet of paper in half horizontally. When folding, leave one side about an inch longer that the other, like the illustration below.

❷ Next, cut the shorter side in half, from the bottom edge up toward the fold. This will result in two flaps on the top part of the paper.

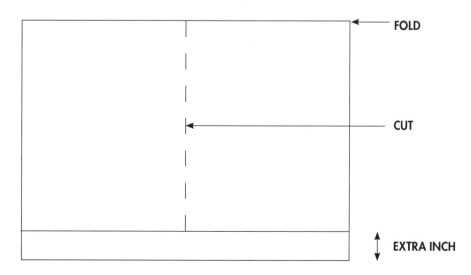

❸ Now students can write and draw the information they need to study on the folded graphic. For example, if using this tool to study a two-step procedure for estimating, the phrase "How to Estimate" can go on the 1 inch section of the bottom. Then, the student can write "First" or "Step One" on the top of the first flap. The second flap should have the word "Second" or the words "Step Two." Write the first step under the first flap and provide an illustration (e.g., Look at the last digit to see if it's 0–4 or 5–9). Under the second flap, write the directions for the second step (e.g., round down for 0–4 and up for 5–9). We have also provided an example Two-Part Folded Graphic used for cause-and-effect relationships.

❹ Students should use their study helpers for independent review, especially when they need to study at home and may not have anyone to help them.

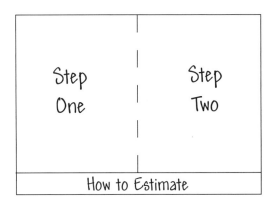

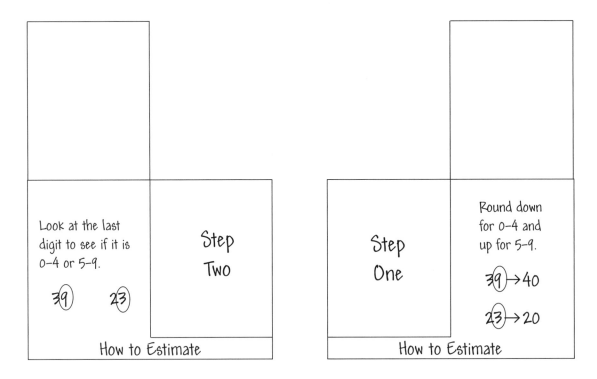

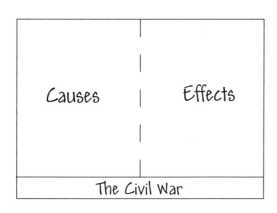

Causes | Effects

The Civil War

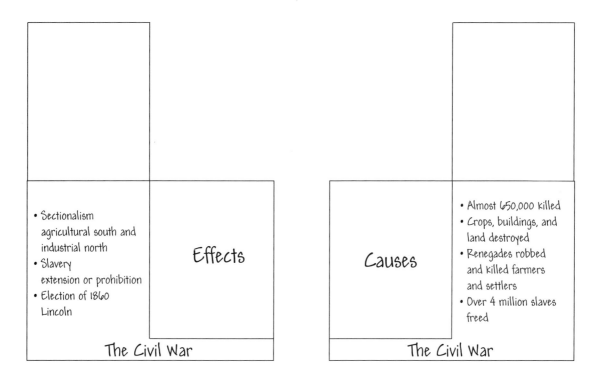

• Sectionalism
  agricultural south and
  industrial north
• Slavery
  extension or prohibition
• Election of 1860
  Lincoln

Effects

The Civil War

Causes

• Almost 650,000 killed
• Crops, buildings, and
  land destroyed
• Renegades robbed
  and killed farmers
  and settlers
• Over 4 million slaves
  freed

The Civil War

Five-Part Folded Graphic

❶ Fold a sheet of paper in half vertically, like the graphic in the illustration.

❷ While holding the folded paper so that the open side of the fold is at the bottom, make four cuts from the bottom edge toward the fold. This will result if five flaps.

❸ Now turn the paper 90 degrees so that you have an $11'' \times 4\frac{1}{4}''$ piece of paper with the fold on the left and the open flaps on the right.

❹ Students can write a vocabulary word, number, step, person's name, or event title on top of each flap. Underneath each flap, students should write the definition, details, or specific directions, along with an illustration.

❺ For independent study, direct students to take this study helper home and check themselves by opening the flaps to see if they wrote or said the correct information.

	Rigid social division based on money, inherited status, race, or religion
	Government by individuals or institution believed to be divinely guided
	Basis is the relationship of lord and servant with all land held in fee
	Undivided rule by a single person
	Citizens vote and have the power

	Rigid social division based on money, inherited status, race, or religion
	Government by individuals or institution believed to be divinely guided
	Basis is the relationship of lord and servant with all land held in fee
	Monarchy
	Citizens vote and have the power

Idea 21
Group Puzzles With a Read-Aloud

Teachers are always looking for effective instructional strategies that are also interactive and enjoyable for students. When several students in a class are struggling to understand content-area material, structuring some group activities allows students to help each other through supportive peer interaction. Group Puzzles With a Read Aloud is a quick strategy that can work for almost any grade level. It uses a jigsaw format to structure teamwork.

Here is how it works.

❶ Before students begin to read their assigned passage, complete the puzzle template by writing questions related to the passage. There are five questions for each group puzzle, beginning with the words, "How," "What," "Where," "When," and "Why." We have also provided a blank puzzle so that you can vary your questions (e.g., you might want to have five "Why" questions for a specific text selection).

❷ After writing the questions you would like students to answer, make a copy for each group. You could also copy the puzzle on a different color of paper for each group. Cut the puzzles apart, but keep the pieces together, either with a clip or in a plastic bag.

❸ Assign students to mixed-ability groups. Each group will need a leader, a coach, and a recorder. The leader will make sure the group remains focused, the coach will help any student who has problems reading aloud, and the recorder will record the group's answers.

❹ Once students are sitting with their assigned group, place the puzzle pieces facedown on each group's table and ask each student to select a question. Each student should read his or her question aloud to the group and then write it on the group record form.

❺ All students in the class should preview the passage by looking at the title, headings, tables, charts, bold or italicized words, illustrations, and other key features.

❻ Each group can then divide the chapter or passage into five sections and determine who will read first, second, third, etc., and how many paragraphs or pages each should read. If groups have trouble splitting up the reading, the leader can make decisions to keep his or her team on track.

➐ Each student reads his or her assigned section of the passage aloud, while other students follow along silently. If the answer to a question is found, any student can speak up and tell the other students which question has been answered and what they think the correct answer is. The recorder should write the answers on the group record form as each is found and agreed upon by the group. By the time the read aloud has ended, the group should have found the answers to all five questions.

➑ If a group finishes reading and is still struggling to find an answer, students can reread sections individually.

➒ When finished, students will submit their group record form for evaluation. After evaluating each group's record form and ensuring accuracy, make five copies and give student one copy of his or her group's answers for later review.

🔖 Tip:

After students are familiar with this process, assign each group a different passage. This will allow the class to cover more material, but it will also require a class discussion and review to ensure individual student's understanding.

Group Puzzles With a Read-Aloud

Record

Names of our group members

_____

_____

_____

_____

_____

Who _____

Answer _____

What _____

Answer _____

Where _____

Answer _____

How _____

Answer _____

Why _____

Answer _____

Idea 21

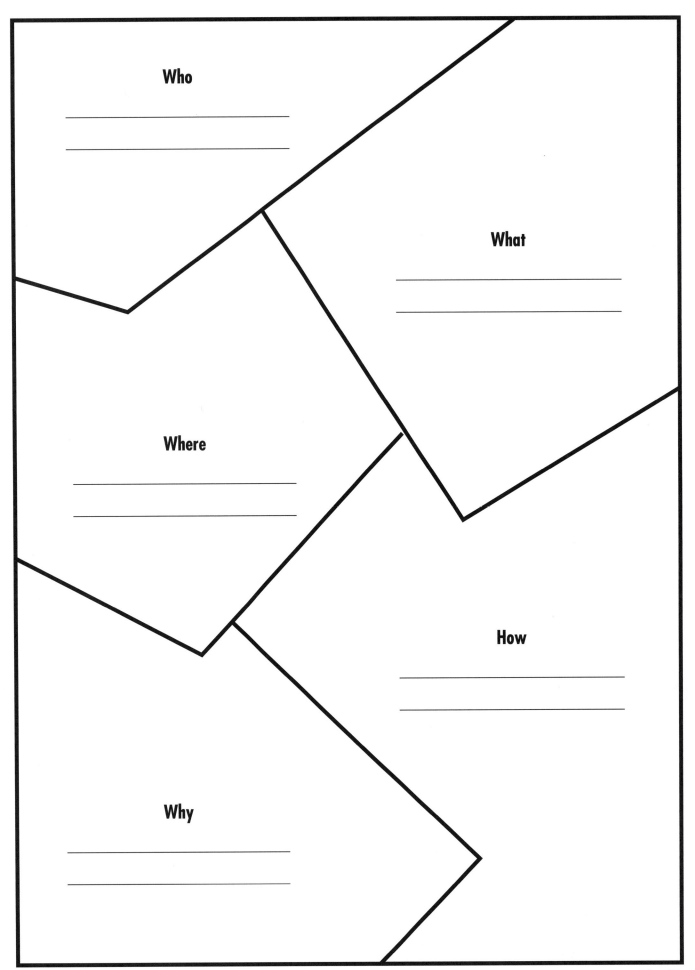

Who

_____

_____

What

_____

_____

Where

_____

_____

How

_____

_____

Why

_____

_____

Idea 21

Idea 22
Ask Your Partner

Ask Your Partner is an easy way to improve students' comprehension and questioning skills. Teach the strategy by modeling and then guiding students as they practice. We have provided a small card that students can use to record the process when they are working in pairs.

Here is how it works.

❶ Assign students to pairs. Put students at similar reading levels in the pairs. Ask students to read a passage (either silently or aloud). When teaching the strategy for young students, the passage can be as short as one or two sentences.

❷ After reading, tell students to close their books and ask their partners at least three questions about the passage. If students have trouble thinking of questions, model for them.

❸ After each partner has asked and answered three questions and checked off the numbers in each column, read the next passage. Repeat the question-and-answer process.

❹ To ensure comprehension, call on individual students to ask and answer questions. Students' grades should be based on both completion of their cards and teacher questioning.

Ask Your Partner

Name _____

Partner's Name _____

Passage Read: page _____ to page _____

Topic _____

Ask your partner three questions about each passage, and cross off a number for each question.

Answer your partner's three questions about each passage, and cross off a number for each answer.

❶
❷
❸

❶
❷
❸

❶
❷
❸

❶
❷
❸

Your Questions

Your Answers

Ask Your Partner

Name _____

Partner's Name _____

Passage Read: page _____ to page _____

Topic _____

Ask your partner three questions about each passage, and cross off a number for each question.

Answer your partner's three questions about each passage, and cross off a number for each answer.

❶
❷
❸

❶
❷
❸

❶
❷
❸

❶
❷
❸

Your Questions

Your Answers

Idea 22

Idea 23

How Do You Know That?

Improving reading comprehension among below-grade-level readers (especially those with learning disabilities) is often a challenge, and even though teachers know how important comprehension skills are, they do not always know specific strategies for improving these skills, especially if they are content-area teachers without a background in reading instruction. Fortunately, there are some strategies for improving students' reading comprehension that are simple and effective. One such strategy is for teachers to ask good questions and to model good thinking in response to those questions. Good questioning techniques help students with conclusions, inferences, main ideas, summarization, and fact versus opinion.

Teachers may wonder how to identify "good" questions and how to "model" thinking. How Do You Know That? is a great idea that should help with both of these issues.

Here is how it works.

❶ When asking students questions about content, don't stop with your first question. After the student has answered your basic informational question, follow up with another question, "How do you know that?"

❷ When using the How Do You Know That? strategy, encourage your students to cite supporting facts and details. If they are struggling, model your own process of "thinking out loud" by saying, "That's correct, (*restate the answer*). We know that because we already learned that (*provide another fact*)."

❸ How Do You Know That? helps students who are just listening, too. Not only do they get to hear the correct answer, but they also get to hear *why* it is correct.

❹ To help yourself remember this strategy, post the cue card so you don't forget to follow up.

Note. This idea is adapted from *Strategies and Tactics for Effective Instruction* (2nd ed.), by B. Algozzine, J. Ysseldyke, and J. Elliott, 1997–1998, Longmont, CO: Sopris West. Copyright 1997–1998 by Bob Algozzine and Jim Ysseldyke. Adapted with permission.

How Do You Know That?

Idea 24
You Versus Me

Here's a great way to review information and challenge your students while having fun. You Versus Me is fast paced and sure to work with students who like to prove to the teacher how much they know. You can really have fun with this idea if you hype it up and get your students excited about beating you.

Here is how it works.

❶ Write an odd number (9 to 15 statements is a good range) of true–false statements about a content-area passage. Ask students to pick a prize they would like if they win the game. Use the prize form provided, or create your own.

❷ After students have read the passage, project one statement at a time onto the board. Quickly read each statement and have the students raise their hands to vote on whether they think the statement is true or false.

❸ The answer that receives the majority of votes is the one that counts. If students are correct, they get a point. If they are incorrect, the teacher gets a point. Record points as tally marks: *You* for students, and *Me* for the teacher.

❹ Whoever has the most points after completing the review wins the game.

You Versus Me Prizes

Pick One

❏ Talk time at the end of class

❏ No homework tonight

❏ Next quiz is open book/open notes

❏ Have class outside during nice weather

❏ Bring a bottle of water to class

❏ Popcorn or pretzels for everyone

❏ Teacher makes dessert for the class and serves it

❏ Music during work time

❏ Reading time (magazines or books)

❏ Work with a partner

❏ Teacher has to sing a song

❏ Get a free 100 quiz grade

Idea 24

Idea 25
Get Different

To measure students' mastery of content-area objectives, teachers should provide a variety of opportunities to demonstrate their learning. If students are given several options for demonstrating mastery, they might be more interested and motivated. We suggest that teachers include product development and production options. Product production encourages students to demonstrate unique, divergent thinking, either individually or as a member of a group. Here is an easy way to ensure that students create a variety of visible products rather than sticking with familiar, commonly used formats.

We have provided several sets of Get Different cards. The cards can be used in making random assignments of products to students. Just shuffle each deck and allow individual students or student groups to pick a card. That way, you make sure that students demonstrate and share their knowledge in many different ways. They learn not just content but several styles of data presentation and a variety of formats in which they can present information.

Make a

Display

Conduct a

Survey

Create an

Experiment

Design a

Game

Create a

Diagram with Labels

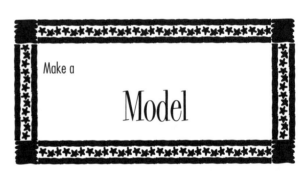

Make a

Model

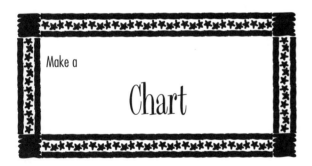

Make a

Chart

Make a

Detailed Illustration

Design a

Web Page

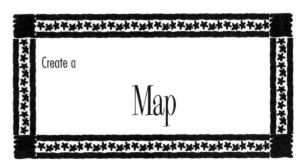

Create a

Map

Idea 25

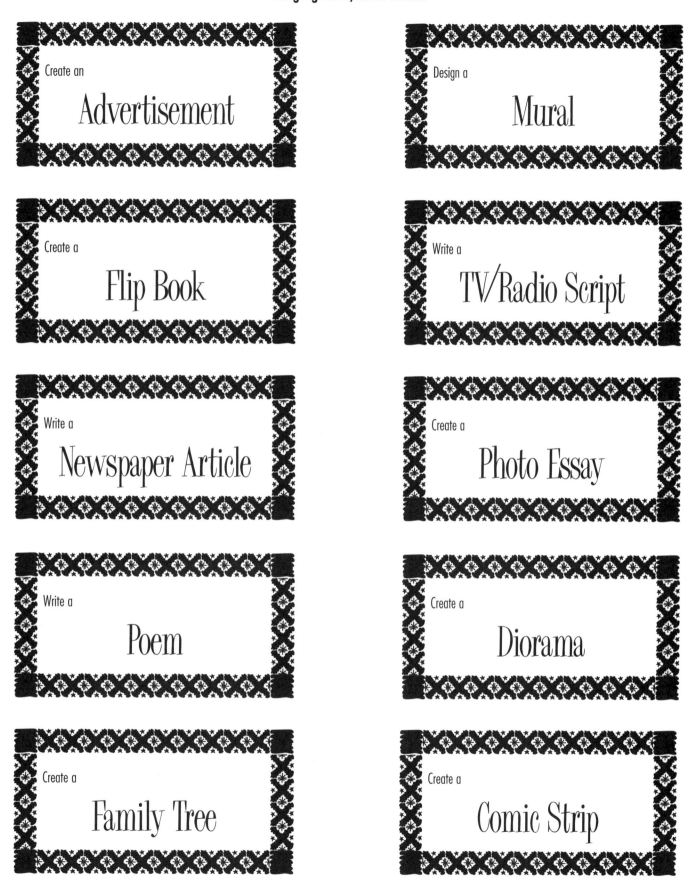

Create an

Advertisement

Design a

Mural

Create a

Flip Book

Write a

TV/Radio Script

Write a

Newspaper Article

Create a

Photo Essay

Write a

Poem

Create a

Diorama

Create a

Family Tree

Create a

Comic Strip

Idea 25

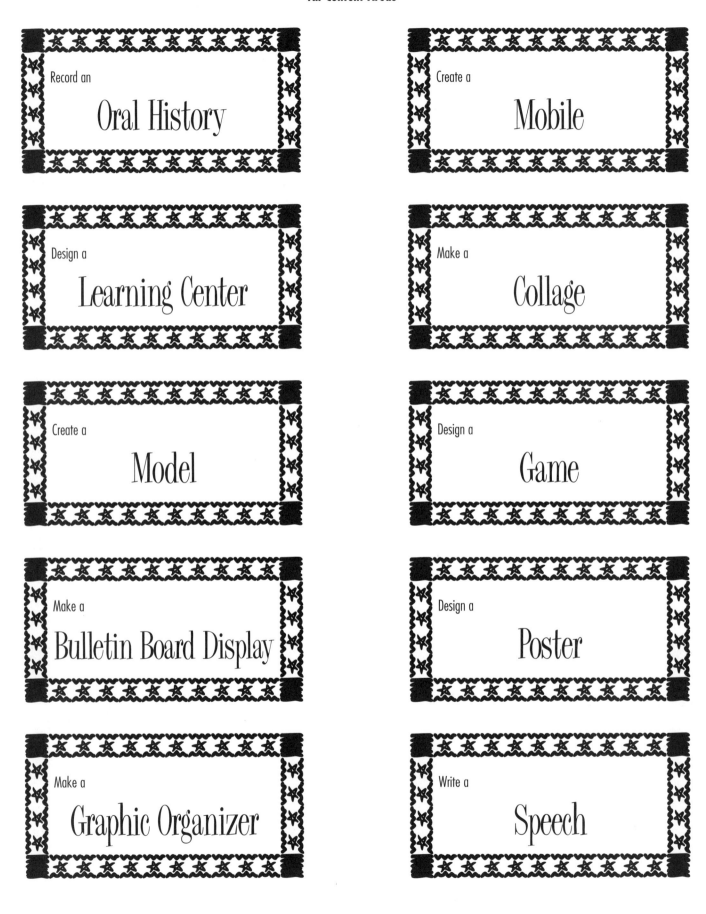

Record an
Oral History

Create a
Mobile

Design a
Learning Center

Make a
Collage

Create a
Model

Design a
Game

Make a
Bulletin Board Display

Design a
Poster

Make a
Graphic Organizer

Write a
Speech

114

Idea 25

115

Idea 26
Graphic Organizers: Reading Comprehension

Graphic organizers help students to understand what they are reading and can be used individually, with partners, or as group activities. It is always important to teach students how to use a graphic organizer. In this idea, we have provided five graphic organizers that can be used with all content areas.

Follow these steps.

❶ Project the blank graphic organizer.

❷ Explain its use by completing the form one or more times.

❸ Show the students several completed examples.

❹ Check students' progress when they first begin using the form.

❺ Ask students to share their completed graphic organizers with the rest of the class.

Instructions

Semantic Webbing

Semantic webbing is a widely used strategy that is effective in helping students extend and deepen their understanding of key concepts, and it can be used with all content areas. To use this form, tell students to write the key concept in the largest rectangle. Write categories that are related to the key concept in the medium-sized rectangles. Finally, complete the web by writing details or related categories in the smallest rectangles. Leave the webs posted on the wall so that students can add to them as they read the text and continue to expand their knowledge.

Charts

Charting information on a topic is a wonderful way to help students organize and make sense of information as they read. The chart provides a focus and reason for reading and helps students know what information is important and needs to be remembered. This strategy is particularly useful in content-area classes. Decide on the important categories of information that reflect the major concepts presented in the material and how those categories can be subdivided. As an advanced organizer, present the chart to students before reading. You can provide each student with an individual copy, duplicate it as an overhead, or make a group-size chart.

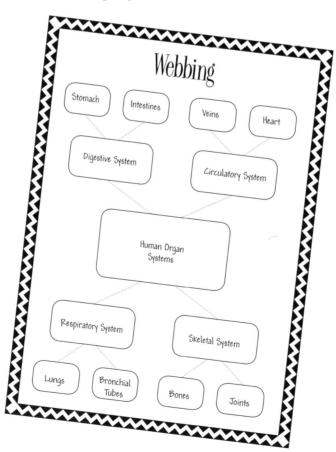

Note. This idea is adapted from *Practical Ideas That Really Work for Students with ADHD: Grade 5 Through Grade 12* (2nd ed.), by K. McConnell and G. R. Ryser, 2005, Austin, TX: PRO-ED. Copyright 2005 by PRO-ED, Inc. Reprinted with permission. [Semantic Webbing (p. 133), Sequence Circle (p. 127), Same/Different (p. 137), Take These Steps (p. 131)]

Sequence Circle

To help students retell a story or the sequence of events in a passage, teach them to write or draw those events on the Sequence Circle. This is a quick and easy tool that helps students see the sequence of events, the relationships among occurrences, and the causes and effects.

Same/Different

The Same/Different form is useful for students as they begin to differentiate and compare two ideas, objects, stories, events, characters, and so on. Students put the names of the two things to be compared in the two boxes at the top (for students who don't write, draw a picture or write the names for them). Next, they list or draw a picture of the differing characteristics or properties of the first thing in the left column and characteristics or properties of the second thing in the right column. Finally, they list or draw a picture of the characteristics the two things have in common in the middle column. Students can use their lists for discussion, writing, and study.

Take These Steps

Take These Steps is a simple form to help students organize information. Have students write information or draw pictures in the boxes and then use the form as a study guide by retracing the steps. This form is great for math problems and science experiments.

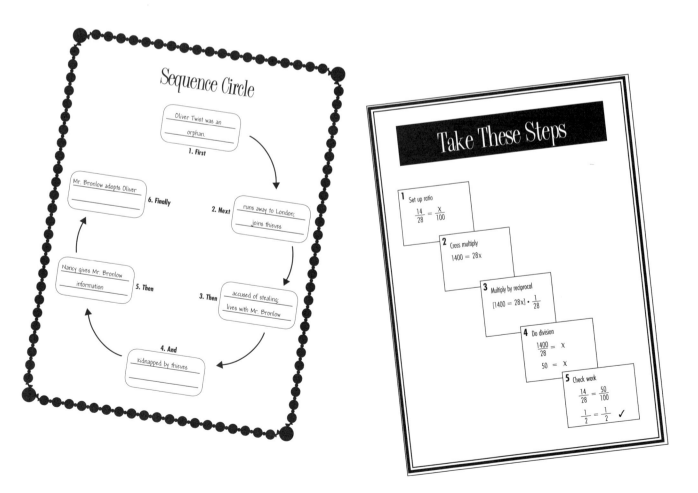

119

Webbing

Idea 26

Webbing

Idea 26

Webbing

Idea 26

Story Characters Chart

Story Title _____

Character	Personality Traits	Actions of Character That Support Traits	Conversation By or About Character That Shows Traits

Idea 26

Literature Chart

Name of Work _____

Setting	Main Characters	Conflict or Action	Theme, Lesson, or Moral

Current or Past Events Chart

Source(s) _____

Date	Event	Person, Country, or Organization	Outcome

Science Experiment Chart

Name of Experiment(s) _____

Hypothesis/ Research Question	Procedures	Results	Conclusion

Math Problem Chart

Type of Problem(s) _____

Problem	Important Information	Operation(s)	Solution

Sequence Circle

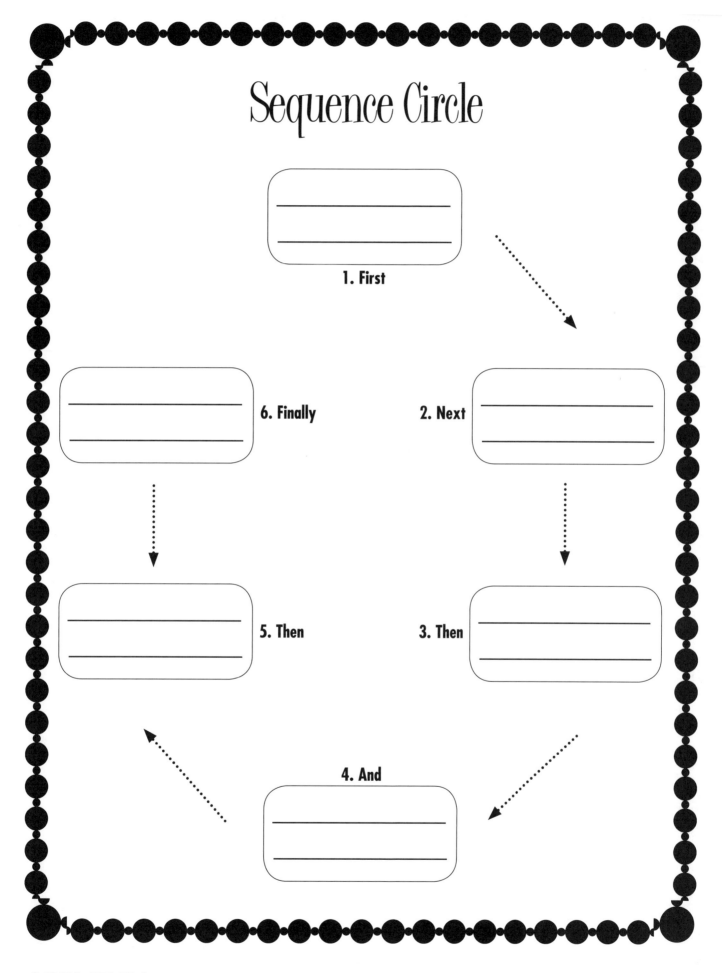

1. First

2. Next

3. Then

4. And

5. Then

6. Finally

Idea 26

Same/Different

1	2
_____	_____

Different	Same	Different

130

Take These Steps

1

2

3

4

5

Idea 26

Take These Steps

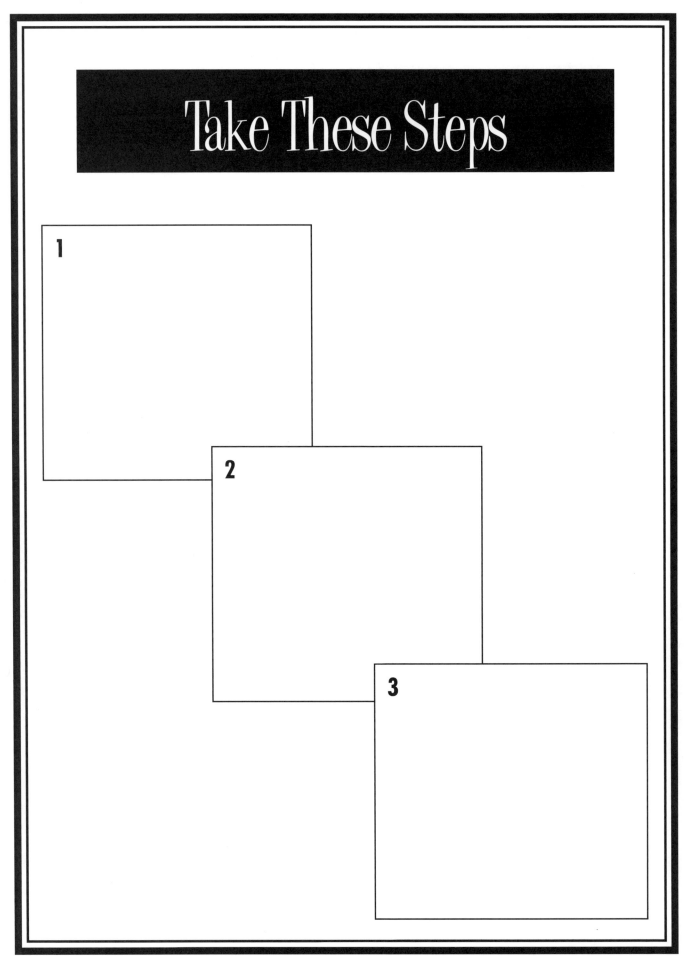

1

2

3

Idea 26

Idea 27
Signal Words

Most content-area textbook material is organized into a particular pattern for each paragraph or section. To help students learn the patterns, teach them the meaning of signal words. Learning the signal words will help them anticipate the text pattern and know what to expect as they read. These signal words are also useful when students are taking tests that require them to read a passage and then answer questions. There are numerous, free sources of signal words available on the Internet. We suggest teaching signal words throughout the school year by combining a variety of teacher and student activities.

Here is how to use this idea.

❶ Provide students a Signal Words chart that includes space for all the pertinent signal-word information they will need. Also, give each student a set of highlighters so that they can practice identifying and highlighting signal words when they see them in text.

❷ Before reading a section of text or other written material, ask students to skim the material and look for the first category of signal word, *Listing*. Students should highlight the listing words in a specified color.

❸ Review with students what this category of signal word means and what they can expect to read after the signal word. Read orally with them, and explain the passage's meaning if they do not understand.

❹ Repeat this process with each of the signal-word categories on the chart, using a specific highlighter color for each one. You may want to add some other categories or signal words that you think are even more useful for students.

❺ Every time students are required to read, remind them to consult their signal-word lists, which should be kept in their notebooks. You can also post a larger version of the charts on the walls of the classroom. When students practice test items, encourage them to look first for signal words. This strategy is easy to use and will help your students know what to expect.

Signal Words

Listing
Category _____

Color _____

What These Signals Mean	Examples			What to Say to Yourself
• Supporting facts or details • No particular order • Equal value or importance	• in addition • another • for example • also • several	• a number of • and • again • likewise • more	• similarly • too • other	Get ready, there are more ideas on the way.

Signal Words

Sequence
Category _____

Color _____

What These Signals Mean	Examples			What to Say to Yourself
• Listed in order they occurred or a specifically planned order • Order is important to the meaning	• first, second, third • in the first place • before, after • until	• when • during • earlier • at last, last	• next • later • A, B, C • now	These ideas are in order. I cannot change the order because it would change the meaning.

© 2009 by PRO-ED, Inc.

134

Idea 27

Compare–Contrast
Category

Signal Words

Color _____

What These Signals Mean	Examples			What to Say to Yourself
• Ideas are related by similarities (compare) or differences (contrast). • The author's purpose is to show these similarities or differences.	• similar, different • on the other hand • but • however • either	• more than, much as • different from • rather • same • although	• while • in the same way • bigger than, smaller than • opposite • though	I am going to read about things that are alike or different now. The author will compare things that are alike and contrast things that are different.

Cause and Effect
Category

Signal Words

Color _____

What These Signals Mean	Examples			What to Say to Yourself
• One event (effect) happened because of some other event, situation, or circumstance (cause). • The cause stimulates the effect.	• because • so that • resulting from • for this reason • consequently	• therefore • on that account • in order that • due to	• since • if, then • thus • so	I am going to read about something that is going to make a change or be changed.

135

Idea 27

Signal Words

Conclusion

Category

Color

What These Signals Mean	Examples			What to Say to Yourself
• End of a discussion • Special importance or emphasis	• as a result • consequently • in conclusion • finally • in summary	• therefore • hence • from this we can see • lastly	• so • above all • most of all • remember that	Okay, here is the end of this reading and it probably has some important information.

Signal Words

Category

Color

What These Signals Mean	Examples			What to Say to Yourself

Idea 27

Idea 28

Look Ahead and Look Back

For students with reading disabilities, textbook material in content-area classes like science, social studies, and math can be challenging to read and to understand. Teachers can help students by preparing them before they read a content-area passage and then reviewing with them after they have completed reading. If done effectively, preparation before reading will give students a "heads up," so they know what information to look for while reading. The review after reading will provide helpful repetition of key ideas and show students how to integrate new information with their prior learning. We have provided a simple form for teachers to use as they help students look ahead and look back.

Here are the steps for using the form.

❶ If the reading is the continuation of a topic already being studied, review prior content and vocabulary; if the reading is the first in a unit of instruction, introduce new vocabulary and brainstorm with students about the topic. Before reading, ask students to look over the pages they are going to read. Focus on the title, headings, bold or italicized words, and any tables, graphs, or other visuals.

❷ Ask students to complete the top of the form and the Look Ahead section. Follow up by asking individual students to share their responses, and complete a version of the form on an electronic white board or overhead transparency. Guide students as they write their three questions to make sure their questions are relevant and important.

❸ Next, students can read the passage either individually or in a whole-class round-robin format, depending on the topic and the students' reading skills.

❹ After reading, students should complete the Look Back section and the one-sentence summary at the bottom of the form.

❺ Either as a large group or in small groups of two to four students, students can discuss their responses and check with their peers for accuracy. Guide students so that they focus on the facts that helped them answer their questions. Model some acceptable one-sentence summaries for students who are having difficulty with this section of the form.

⬥ Give your students feedback so that they know which answers are acceptable. Sometimes, several different responses may be correct; other times, there might be only one right answer to a question. Students should keep their completed forms in their notebooks so that they have accurate information to study before a test or quiz or to use in a written assignment.

Look Ahead and Look Back

Title/Topic ___Huckleberry Finn, by Mark Twain___ Page Numbers ___24–43___

What do I expect to learn? ___What happens to Huck after Pap doesn't let him go to school___

What do I already know about this topic? ___Huck's Pap has locked him up in a cabin in the woods.___

Look Ahead (Before Reading)

What do I think is the main idea of this reading?

Sometimes you have to take care of yourself.

Questions I want answered about the topic are

❶ Did Huck escape from the cabin?

❷ Did Huck want to return to civilization?

❸ Why was Pap so prejudiced?

Look Back (After Reading)

Was I right about the main idea? If not, what is the main idea?

Yes. Also, Huck believes in treating everyone with kindness.

Answers to my questions are

❶ Yes.

❷ Not at first, but after Pap beat him, he did.

❸ He was poor and uneducated and maybe blamed others.

Here is my one sentence summary of the reading.

Pap was poor and uneducated and wanted to keep Huck the same, so Huck knew he had to escape to have a chance at life.

Look Ahead and Look Back

Title/Topic _____

Page Numbers _____

What do I expect to learn? _____

What do I already know about this topic? _____

Look Ahead *(Before Reading)*

What do I think is the main idea of this reading?

_____

_____

Questions I want answered about the topic are

❶ _____

❷ _____

❸ _____

Look Back *(After Reading)*

Was I right about the main idea? If not, what is the main idea?

_____

_____

Answers to my questions are

❶ _____

❷ _____

❸ _____

Here is my one sentence summary of the reading.

_____

139

Idea 28

Idea 29

Five, Four, Three

Many students have difficulty understanding the reading material in content-area classes. Students who are not reading at their grade level might struggle so much that they finish reading but do not comprehend what they read. For these and other students, use the Five, Four, Three idea, which uses group strategies to activate prior knowledge but requires students to read and answer questions individually.

Here is how to use the form.

❶ Each student should complete the first two lines that ask for the topic and sections to be read.

❷ In the first box, all students, with the help of the teacher, should generate a main question about the reading. This can be based on a preview of the title, headings, illustrations, and vocabulary.

❸ To complete the Five Facts We Already Know box, the whole class should brainstorm a list of at least five things they already know about the topic. Each student should record these facts.

❹ Students should write down four key vocabulary words in the Four Key Vocabulary Words box. If these words are unfamiliar to students, use some of the strategies in the vocabulary section of this manual to teach the words' definitions.

❺ To complete the questions part of the form, each student should work individually to think of three more questions about the topic. Review students' questions in a group discussion.

❻ Students will read the passage, stopping occasionally as they find the answers to their three specific questions. When they find an answer, they should write both the answer and the page where they found it.

❼ After students have completed their questions and answers, the group can review each other's responses, either in small groups or in a large-group discussion.

Five, Four, Three

Topic _____

Pages/Section of Reading _____

Our Main Question

_____

Five Facts We Already Know

❶ _____

❷ _____

❸ _____

❹ _____

❺ _____

Four Key Vocabulary Words

❶ _____

❷ _____

❸ _____

❹ _____

Three Questions	**Three Answers**	**Page**
❶ _____	❶ _____	_____
❷ _____	❶ _____	_____
❸ _____	❶ _____	_____

Idea 29

Idea 30

Team Brain Writing

One way to boost interest and help students link prior knowledge to current instruction in content-area classes is brainstorming. Although most teachers are familiar with traditional brainstorming, which involves an "all verbal" format, we have a different brainstorming strategy to suggest. Team Brain Writing requires students to brainstorm ideas silently, then discuss, evaluate, and select their best ideas verbally, as members of a team.

Here is how Team Brain Writing works.

❶ Divide your students into teams. You can use larger or smaller teams, but four is a manageable number for the average class.

❷ Write one question or problem statement ("How could we . . .?" "What would improve . . .?" "What would work for . . .?") at the top of each form, then duplicate the forms so that each team will receive the same set of four questions. These questions or problem statements should be open ended and related to the upcoming topic.

❸ Ask the team members to sit facing each other. Make sure each student has a pen or pencil for writing and that there is a clear workspace for the team.

❹ The directions for students follow: "You have four pieces of paper in front of you on the table. Each paper has a question or problem statement on it. You have 15 minutes to write solutions, answers, and ideas in response to the questions. Write as quickly as you can. You may read others' ideas, but do not talk. Try to write several ideas on each piece of paper. After writing an idea on one piece of paper, put that paper back in the center of the table, take another one, and write another idea. Repeat as often as you can in 15 minutes."

❺ When the 15-minute period is up, ask students to review each question or problem statement. One student in each team should read the ideas related to each specific question.

Note. This idea is from *Practical Ideas That Really Work for Secondary Students in Inclusive Classrooms* (pp. 25–30), by K. McConnell and G. R. Ryser, 2007, Austin, TX: PRO-ED, Inc. Copyright 2007 by PRO-ED, Inc. Reprinted with permission.

⬦ Have the students discuss and evaluate. In their small-team groups, students should talk about the advantages and disadvantages of each response, eliminate responses that are duplicate ideas, combine responses that are related, and select their favorites. This stage of Team Brain Writing should take about 20 minutes.

⬦ In a large-group discussion, give each team an opportunity to talk about their best ideas—what they think would really work to solve a problem or improve a situation.

⬦ Later, as the class studies the new topic, revisit the problem statements, remind students of their original ideas, and link them to current the discussions.

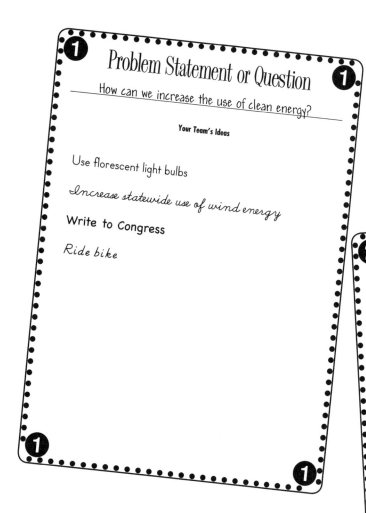

Problem Statement or Question

How can we increase the use of clean energy?

Your Team's Ideas

Use florescent light bulbs

Increase statewide use of wind energy

Write to Congress

Ride bike

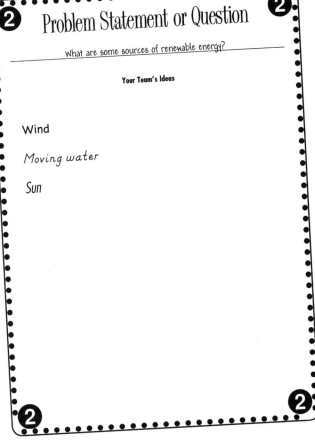

Problem Statement or Question

What are some sources of renewable energy?

Your Team's Ideas

Wind

Moving water

Sun

Problem Statement or Question

_____

Your Team's Ideas

Idea 30

Problem Statement or Question

_____

Your Team's Ideas

Idea 30

Problem Statement or Question

_____

Your Team's Ideas

147

Problem Statement or Question

_____

Your Team's Ideas

Idea 30

Idea 31
Look for Clues

If students pay attention to the clues or signals in surrounding text, they will often be able to make an educated guess and figure out the meaning of an unknown or unfamiliar word. This strategy of using context clues to determine a word's meaning is an efficient way for students to increase understanding without resorting to breaking the word into parts or using a dictionary. The use of context clues will also help students as they read increasingly challenging text.

In the Look for Clues form, we have provided information on the four most common context clues, including a synonym or restatement, an explanation or definition, an antonym, and an example. We have also provided information about the punctuation used in sentences, which is another strategy for determining word meaning.

The Look for Clues form can be the basis for teaching students how to use context clues independently as they read—but just giving students the form is not enough. You should directly teach students how to use context clues and give them many opportunities to rehearse and practice. Periodically review their use and reteach as necessary.

Here is how to teach students to Look for Clues.

❶ Provide specific examples of each type of clue, and then model how to use them using a *think aloud* process. For each type of context clue, write three to five example sentences that are at the students' reading level, each containing an unknown word. Read each sentence aloud. For example, your first sentence might be, "The principal made Grant *relinquish* his cell phone, because students are not allowed to have them in school." As you read the sentence, emphasize the unknown word.

❷ Depending on the age and reading level of your students, you could also leave out the unknown word as you read the sentence and say, "blank" in its place. For example, "The principal made Grant *blank* his cell phone, because students are not allowed to have them in school."

❸ Model your think aloud as you point out clues and ask yourself questions. You might begin by saying, "I have read the sentence, but I don't know what *relinquish* means. But look, there is the phrase that might explain the meaning. The sentence says, '. . . because students are not allowed to have them in school.' If students are not allowed to have cell phones in school, maybe the principal made Grant *give it up*. So maybe *relinquish* means to have to give something up or stop holding it. Does that make sense?"

❹ Finally, model a read aloud of the sentence again and ask students if the meaning of the word fits the sentence. For example, you would say aloud, "The principal made Grant give up and stop holding his cell phone because students are not allowed to have them in school." See if students agree that the meaning fits the context of the sentence.

It will be important for students to practice using context clues with your guidance. Only if you provide opportunities for practice and then check students' understanding will you know if they can use the strategies as they read independently. After providing several example sentences for each type of context clue and modeling a think aloud for each, provide some sentences that have each type of clue but are in random order. Ask students to tell you which type of clue is in the sentence(s) and then guess at the meaning of the unknown word.

✿ Tip:

Another way to introduce students to context clues is to write sentences with nonsense words and let them use the chart to figure out what each nonsense word means. The process works just like the steps in Look for Clues, but with nonsense words.

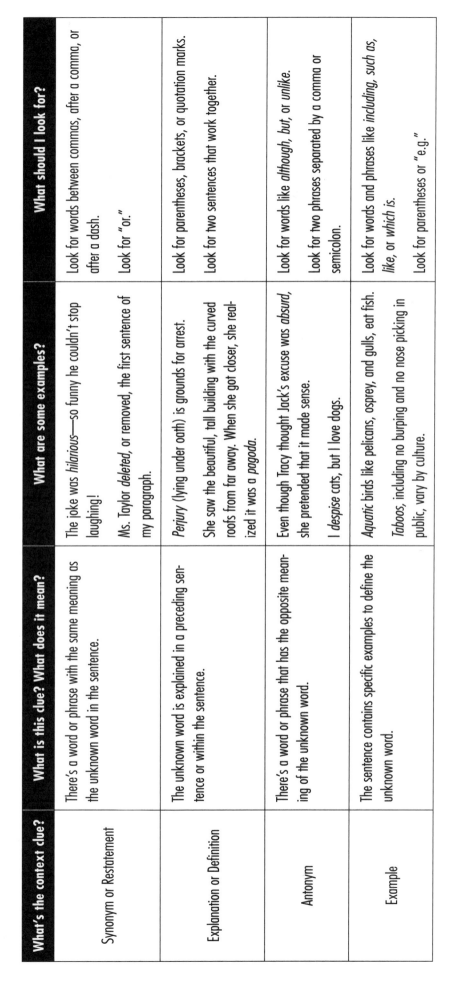

Look for Clues

What's the context clue?	What is this clue? What does it mean?	What are some examples?	What should I look for?
Synonym or Restatement	There's a word or phrase with the same meaning as the unknown word in the sentence.	The joke was *hilarious*—so funny he couldn't stop laughing! Ms. Taylor *deleted*, or removed, the first sentence of my paragraph.	Look for words between commas, after a comma, or after a dash. Look for "or."
Explanation or Definition	The unknown word is explained in a preceding sentence or within the sentence.	*Perjury* (lying under oath) is grounds for arrest. She saw the beautiful, tall building with the curved roofs from far away. When she got closer, she realized it was a *pagoda*.	Look for parentheses, brackets, or quotation marks. Look for two sentences that work together.
Antonym	There's a word or phrase that has the opposite meaning of the unknown word.	Even though Tracy thought Jack's excuse was *absurd*, she pretended that it made sense. I *despise* cats, but I love dogs.	Look for words like *although*, *but*, or *unlike*. Look for two phrases separated by a comma or semicolon.
Example	The sentence contains specific examples to define the unknown word.	*Aquatic* birds like pelicans, osprey, and gulls, eat fish. *Taboos*, including no burping and no nose picking in public, vary by culture.	Look for words and phrases like *including*, *such as*, *like*, or *which is*. Look for parentheses or "e.g."

Idea 31

Idea 32

Keep On Reading

Teachers can expose students to a large amount of unfamiliar vocabulary prior to reading new text material, but it is impossible to teach every new, unknown word students need to know. Students must be able to make good educated guesses about some words' definitions if they are to become efficient, independent readers. Keep On Reading is a simple strategy that can help students learn the meanings of unknown words through context clues, but, for many students, it must be directly taught, modeled, and practiced.

Here is how this idea works.

❶ When introducing students to a new unit of instruction, a reading passage, or other content material, give them a Keep On Reading form with 5 to 10 unfamiliar words listed in the first column that they will need to know as they master the material.

❷ Ask students to predict the meanings of the words, based on their background knowledge, their knowledge of word structures, and their prior exposure to similar words. If the first word is *flotilla,* which means "a fleet of ships or a large force of moving things" (Webster's dictionary), students might relate the word to *float* and suggest that it means something that floats. Record all predictions of its definition, and keep the list visible as students read.

❸ Present students with a short section of their reading, and ask them to skim it to see if any of the new vocabulary words can be found in this section. If so, highlight those words on the form. We found the word *flotilla* in an essay by Stephen Harrigan called "The Secret Life of the Beach" (Harrigan, 1988).

❹ Model for students how to Keep On Reading by reading the entire sentence with the first new word aloud. In our example, the complete sentence is, "Beyond the outermost bar, however, is a large flotilla of these creatures, their purple sacs driven by the wind across the surface of the water." Again, ask students to predict the meaning of the word. Cross off the recorded definitions that were initially predicted but no longer make sense, and add any new definitions that students have thought of, based on the context clues.

5 Read the sentence with the word *blank* inserted in place of the new word. For example, "Beyond the outermost bar, however, is a large *blank* of these creatures, their purple sacs driven by the wind across the surface of the water." Again, ask students if they can suggest a definition that makes sense. By now, it is likely that they have suggested a meaning that is close to the actual meaning of the word.

6 Read the sentence for the third time, substituting one of the words from the students' list (i.e., their best guess at the definition for the word). For example, "Beyond the outermost bar, however, is a large floating group of these creatures, their purple sacs driven by the wind across the surface of the water." If their guess is correct, as in our example, congratulate your students and move on to the next word and the next passage.

7 If students have not yet guessed the meaning, keep reading. Read the sentence before the sentence with the word, the sentence with the word, and the next sentence, all of which have clues to the definition of *flotilla*.

> There are other men-of-war in the surf, helpless to control their fate in the choppy waves. Beyond the outermost bar, however, is a large flotilla of these creatures, their purples sacs driven by the wind across the surface of the water. The men-of-war are not individual animals, they are strange aggregates of other organisms, all of them too highly specialized to exist on their own.

8 After reading sentences before and after the sentence containing the new word, point out and discuss additional context clues. In our example, the phrase *not individual animals*, the location of the men-of-war (in the surf), and the word *large* all provide additional context clues that should suggest the meaning of *flotilla*. In some content material, there may also be pictures, headings, charts, or other context clues. Encourage students to visualize as they read. For example, picturing in their mind the men-of-war in a large group floating.

9 For the last time, if necessary, ask students to take their best guess at the definition of the unknown word. If they get it, congratulate them, and ask them to write the definition on their form. If not, tell them the definition, and then model the process again with the next word.

Give your students Keep On Reading cue cards to remind them of the steps when they work independently.

This process should be practiced, and teachers should make an effort to include all students, requiring each to suggest a meaning at some point in the reading process. While the strategy may seem time-consuming at first, most students will learn it quickly. Keep practicing, and your students will soon begin to master new vocabulary on their own.

Note. The example for this idea is based on an excerpt from "The Secret Life of the Beach," by S. Harrigan, 1988, from *A Natural State. Essays on Texas,* pp. 33–50. Austin, TX: University of Texas Press.

Keep On Reading

New Words   **Meanings**

1. _____   1. _____
                                                         _____
2. _____   2. _____
                                                         _____
3. _____   3. _____
                                                         _____
4. _____   4. _____
                                                         _____
5. _____   5. _____
                                                         _____
6. _____   6. _____
                                                         _____
7. _____   7. _____
                                                         _____
8. _____   8. _____
                                                         _____
9. _____   9. _____
                                                         _____
10. _____   10. _____
                                                         _____

Idea 32

Keep On Reading

1. New words

2. What I think they mean

3. Read passage (highlight new words)

4. New predicted meaning (If different now)

5. Read highlighted words as *blank*

6. Read sentences with my meanings

7. If still not sure, read sentences before and after

Keep On Reading

1. New words

2. What I think they mean

3. Read passage (highlight new words)

4. New predicted meaning (If different now)

5. Read highlighted words as *blank*

6. Read sentences with my meanings

7. If still not sure, read sentences before and after

Keep On Reading

1. New words

2. What I think they mean

3. Read passage (highlight new words)

4. New predicted meaning (If different now)

5. Read highlighted words as *blank*

6. Read sentences with my meanings

7. If still not sure, read sentences before and after

Keep On Reading

1. New words

2. What I think they mean

3. Read passage (highlight new words)

4. New predicted meaning (If different now)

5. Read highlighted words as *blank*

6. Read sentences with my meanings

7. If still not sure, read sentences before and after

Idea 32

Idea 33

Check Yourselves

Checklists can help students evaluate their use of reading strategies. We have provided a checklist that will help your students check themselves after they read. The Reading Strategies Self-Check asks the student to check Yes or No to evaluate their use of specific strategies.

Follow these steps.

❶ Model the use of these reading strategies with a sample reading passage.

❷ Demonstrate how to use each strategy.

❸ Provide opportunities for practice.

❹ When you are comfortable that your students understand the process, let them begin to evaluate their own use of the strategies. Guide them individually and in small groups until they are comfortable and are examining their reading skills with a constructively critical eye.

Reading Strategies Self-Check

Did you make a prediction about the reading passage? ☐ Yes ☐ No

Did you read the headings, illustrations, and key words
to get the main idea? ☐ Yes ☐ No

Did you scan the passage? ☐ Yes ☐ No

Did you make notes in the margins, underline, or highlight? ☐ Yes ☐ No

Did you stop and visualize, creating a picture in your head? ☐ Yes ☐ No

---

Reading Strategies Self-Check

Did you make a prediction about the reading passage? ☐ Yes ☐ No

Did you read the headings, illustrations, and key words
to get the main idea? ☐ Yes ☐ No

Did you scan the passage? ☐ Yes ☐ No

Did you make notes in the margins, underline, or highlight? ☐ Yes ☐ No

Did you stop and visualize, creating a picture in your head? ☐ Yes ☐ No

Idea 34

10-Minute Review Out Loud

For students who are struggling, understanding text they have read can be difficult, and summarizing a selection they have read can be even more of a challenge. However, summarization can improve comprehension if the words used in the summary are simpler than the text and if students can listen to and learn from their peers.

The 10-Minute Review Out Loud is a step-by-step way to summarize that is great for secondary students. This strategy can be used by the whole class.

Here are the steps.

❶ Select a short section for students to read. Because students will be highlighting or underlining as they read, make photocopies of the reading instead of using the textbook. The total time spent reading during the 10-Minute Review Out Loud is about 5 minutes, so select a passage that can be read in that amount of time.

❷ Ask students to read silently. Tell them to underline or highlight key words, phrases, or sentences in the selection as they read. Stop promptly after 2 minutes, and tell the students to turn their papers facedown.

❸ Ask students to tell you what the selection they read was about (i.e., rephrase it in their own words). As students tell you the ideas presented in the selection they read, record them on a whiteboard, chart tablet, or overhead transparency. Make sure you keep your summary sentences short, and write so that everyone in the class can see them. This step should also take about 2 minutes.

❹ Tell your students to turn their papers over and begin to read again. Students who did not finish reading the entire selection the first time should pick up where they stopped. Students who read quickly can reread the selection. Again, at the end of 2 minutes, ask students to stop reading and turn their papers facedown on their desks.

Note. This idea is from *Practical Ideas That Really Work for English Language Learners* (pp. 125–127), by K. McConnell, D. Campos, and G. R. Ryser, 2006, Austin, TX: PRO-ED. Copyright 2006 by PRO-ED, Inc. Reprinted with permission.

5 Read the students' summarization statements aloud, and then ask them to fill in the gaps. Ask questions like, "Are there any key points we missed the first time?" "Is there anything you think we should add, based on your second reading of the material?" "What else should be included in the summary?" Take about 1 minute for this step.

6 For the last reading, allow students 1 minute. Tell them to read quickly this time, focusing on the title, illustrations, key words, and their underlined phrases and sentences.

7 After students have finished reading for the third and final time, review with them the summarization sentences on the board or overhead. During this review, number the sentences with a bright-colored marker. Put a number 1 in front of the main idea, cross out redundant ideas, and link similar thoughts with lines or arrows. This should take about 1 minute.

8 Ask students to do a 1-minute summary. Assign each student a partner. With his or her partner, each student should summarize what they have read. Students can look at the board or overhead as they summarize. The total time for partners to summarize should be about 1 minute.

By the time this process is completed, in about 10 minutes, students will have had three opportunities to read and will have heard the information in the selection restated at least three times. For students who would not have understood the material on their own, 10-Minute Review Out Loud is a great way to boost their comprehension. We have provided cue cards for students to use as reminders of the process.

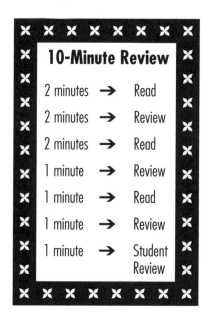

10-Minute Review

2 minutes	→	Read
2 minutes	→	Review
2 minutes	→	Read
1 minute	→	Review
1 minute	→	Read
1 minute	→	Review
1 minute	→	Student Review

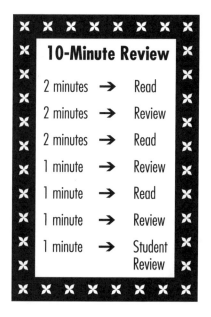

10-Minute Review

2 minutes	→	Read
2 minutes	→	Review
2 minutes	→	Read
1 minute	→	Review
1 minute	→	Read
1 minute	→	Review
1 minute	→	Student Review

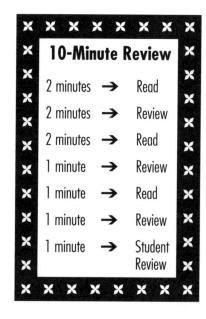

10-Minute Review

2 minutes	→	Read
2 minutes	→	Review
2 minutes	→	Read
1 minute	→	Review
1 minute	→	Read
1 minute	→	Review
1 minute	→	Student Review

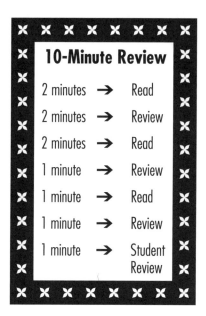

10-Minute Review

2 minutes	→	Read
2 minutes	→	Review
2 minutes	→	Read
1 minute	→	Review
1 minute	→	Read
1 minute	→	Review
1 minute	→	Student Review

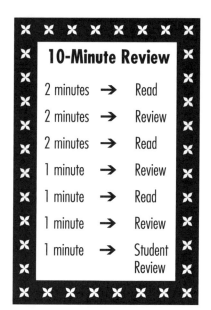

10-Minute Review

2 minutes	→	Read
2 minutes	→	Review
2 minutes	→	Read
1 minute	→	Review
1 minute	→	Read
1 minute	→	Review
1 minute	→	Student Review

10-Minute Review

2 minutes	→	Read
2 minutes	→	Review
2 minutes	→	Read
1 minute	→	Review
1 minute	→	Read
1 minute	→	Review
1 minute	→	Student Review

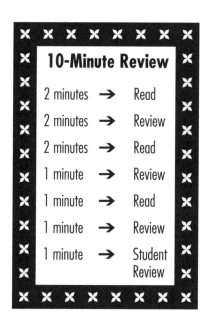

10-Minute Review

2 minutes	→	Read
2 minutes	→	Review
2 minutes	→	Read
1 minute	→	Review
1 minute	→	Read
1 minute	→	Review
1 minute	→	Student Review

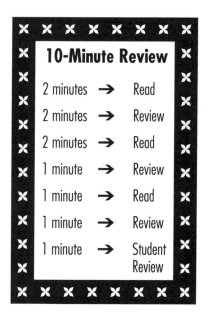

10-Minute Review

2 minutes	→	Read
2 minutes	→	Review
2 minutes	→	Read
1 minute	→	Review
1 minute	→	Read
1 minute	→	Review
1 minute	→	Student Review

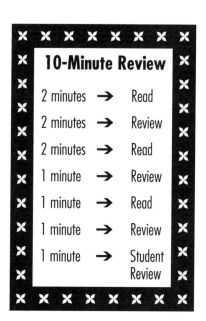

10-Minute Review

2 minutes	→	Read
2 minutes	→	Review
2 minutes	→	Read
1 minute	→	Review
1 minute	→	Read
1 minute	→	Review
1 minute	→	Student Review

Idea 34

Idea 35
Thinking, Cubed

Students with reading problems often have difficulty discussing a character or conflict in literature or an issue or problem in a content-area subject. This idea uses a cube to help students discuss and think about a character, issue, or problem from many angles. Each side of the cube contains a discussion point or question stem about the topic under study. The sides of the cube should balance the levels of Bloom's taxonomy to ensure that students of different ability levels have the opportunity to contribute.

Here is how this idea works.

❶ Use the provided cube template to make the die.

❷ Select a topic and paste a discussion point or question stem on each side of the cube. For reading or English, focus on character development or story conflict. For content-area classes, focus on cause and effect, analysis of social trends, or development of hypotheses. Examples have been provided for you.

❸ Divide students into groups of 3 or 4. Choose or have students choose a recorder for each group. The first student rolls the die and attempts to address the discussion point or answer the question. His or her ideas are recorded and the next student rolls the die. If the student rolls the same discussion point or question stem, he or she adds to the first student's responses.

❹ Repeat the process until every student has had at least one turn rolling the die and responding.

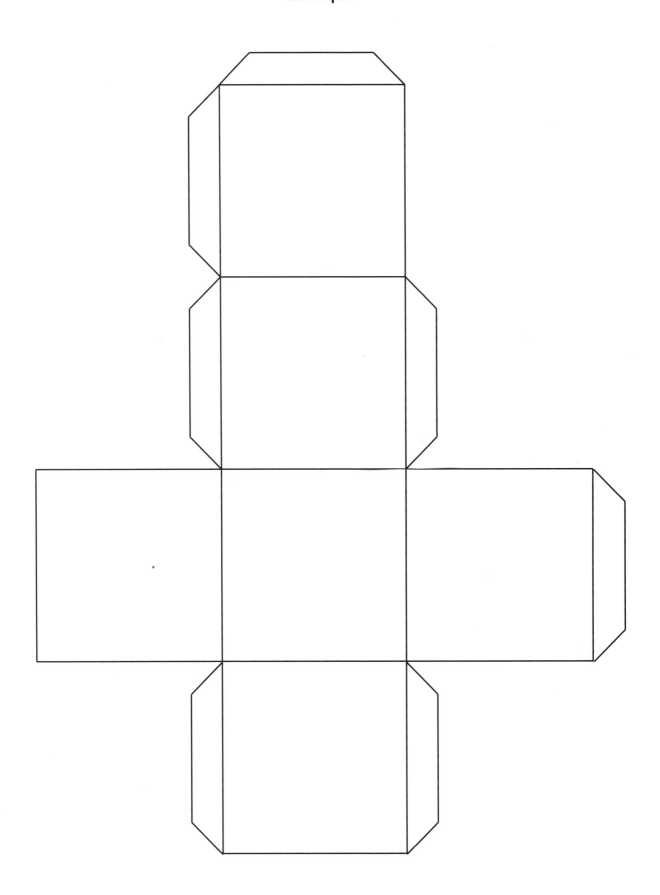

Idea 35

Stems for Literature

Identify the main character and the setting of the story.

Talk about another character we have read about and the differences to the main character of this story.

Predict what might happen to the character after the book ends.

Describe the problem faced by the main character.

Choose a different time frame for the story, and tell what might be different.

Do you agree with the character's decisions in solving the problem?

What would you have done differently?

Stems for Social Studies

Identify three causes for _____.

Who were the two most influential people in achieving _____.

Why do you believe that?

Name two people we read about in this chapter.

Identify one contribution or action of each character.

Identify two effects of _____.

Why do you think that the city/area of _____ was important at this time in history?

What is a _____?

Idea 35

Stems for Science

What is a
_____?

The main reason that
_____ happens
is _____.

Why is _____
important in maintaining
_____?

Identify two characteristics
of _____.

If _____ happened,
what would be the
possible effect?

Can you think of something
in your life that is similar to
_____?

Stems for Any Subject Using Bloom's Taxonomy

What is _____?

(Recall)

Use this information to
predict_____?

(Application)

What would happen if
_____ changed
to _____?

(Synthesis)

Why did _____
happen?

(Comprehension)

How many _____ are
related to _____?

How do you know?

(Analysis)

Rank all possible outcomes
of _____
in priority order.

(Evaluation)

166

Idea 35

Idea 36
Become a Techie

For teachers who want to maximize instructional impact for students who have reading disabilities, technology offers an almost endless selection of multimedia resources in all subject areas. Many students who have difficulties in reading benefit from visual and audio instruction. When this type of instruction is available on the Internet, students can often learn at their own pace, repeat sections of instruction that they did not understand the first time, and have access to real-life examples in specific subject areas.

By doing an Internet search with terms like *audio-video teaching resources, learning technology resources, video learning,* or specific subject area terms and other descriptors, teachers can find a wealth of resources that can benefit students with reading disabilities.

Here are some technology options.

❶ Videoconferencing ideas and training are available for presentation skills, classroom design, and lesson planning. These resources help teachers who want to use more technology when they teach.

❷ Streaming technology provides tutorials, online magazines, and video clips that help students connect to text material.

❸ Distance learning opportunities are provided to schools through libraries, universities, instructional networks, and virtual schools.

❹ Magazines offer content related to news events, current issues, lists of trends and products, and free resources for teachers.

❺ Newsgroups, blogs, and e-mail lists can provide opportunities for discussions, interactive videoconferencing, and forums related to specific subjects.

While we do not endorse any specific Web site and recommend that school districts and teachers constantly monitor Internet content, we found the following examples of technology resources through a quick Internet search.

Here are a few Web sites.

⊙ www.onlinemathlearning.com offers math help, games, and SAT or ACT practice. Users must register.

⊙ www.edutopia.org is a site for teachers and students. Examples of topics and links include *Project-Based Learning: At a Glance, Parent Involvement,* and *Assessment.*

⊙ www.unitedstreaming.com is a commercial service that charges a subscription rate to provide video clips for use in classrooms. These video clips provide real-life visual examples for students who may lack prior knowledge about a topic.

⊙ Distance learning consortiums and communities like DIAL (Distance Interactive Learning) in South Dakota (www.sddial.k12.sd.us) offer teacher lesson plans and Web links by content area and grade.

⊙ www.eduscapes.com provides resources for topics students and teachers would like to research, online learning, and a variety of resources on other topics. Multimedia Seeds, which started as a university course, can be accessed by anyone who wants to learn about using multimedia more effectively.

⊙ www.eschoolnews.com is a Web site that provides resources, reports, and links to other educational technology sites.

As technological innovations become more widely available, teachers in all geographic locations and any size school district will be able to make learning experiences more relevant, meaningful, and accessible for students with and without disabilities.

Idea 37
Graphic Organizers: Metacognitive Skills

Graphic organizers can help students become more proficient readers and can be used individually, with partners, or as group activities. In this idea, we have provided two graphic organizers that can be used in all content areas.

Follow these steps.

❶ Project the blank graphic organizer.

❷ Explain how it is used by completing the form.

❸ Show the students several completed examples.

❹ Check students' progress when they begin using the form.

❺ Ask students to share their completed graphic organizers with the rest of the class.

Instructions

I See Your Point of View

One of the most difficult tasks for students to do is interpret a reading passage from multiple points of view. This is especially important when studying current events or great literature. Teaching students to interpret readings from multiple points of view gives them a purpose for reading.

Think Sheet

We can improve students' comprehension of content text by helping them monitor their own understanding as they read. Do this by teaching them to ask questions about what they are reading and then to make inferences from the text to answer their own questions. Students record what they learned from a reading in the *I Learned* column, questions they have about what they read in the *I Wonder* column, and answers or inferences to the questions in the *I Infer* column.

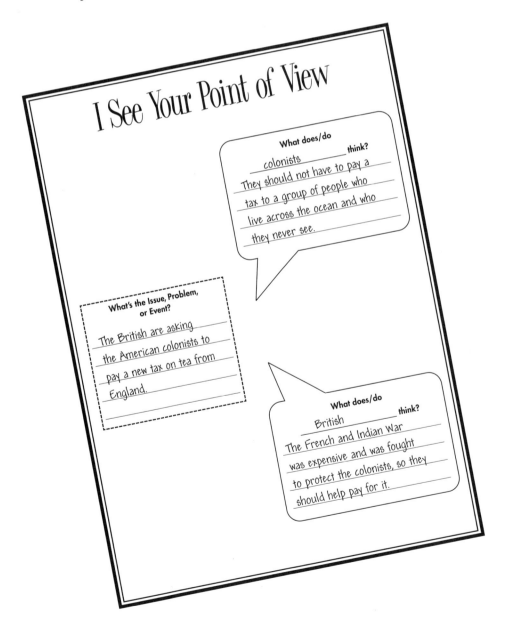

I See Your Point of View

What does/do

_____ **think?**

_____

_____

_____

_____

What's the Issue, Problem, or Event?

_____

_____

_____

_____

_____

What does/do

_____ **think?**

_____

_____

_____

_____

Idea 37

I See Your Point of View

What does/do

_____ think?

_____

_____

_____

What's the Issue, Problem, or Event?

_____

_____

_____

_____

_____

_____

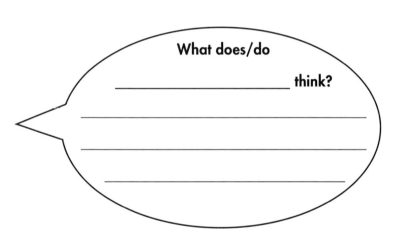

What does/do

_____ think?

_____

_____

_____

What does/do

_____ think?

_____

_____

_____

Idea 37

Think Sheet

Reading Passage _____

I Learned . . .	I Wonder . . .	I Infer . . .

Idea 37